To Be Nsala's Daughter

To Be Nsala's Daughter

Decomposing the Colonial Gaze

CHÉRIE N. RIVERS

DUKE UNIVERSITY PRESS · DURHAM AND LONDON · 2023

Printed in the United States of America on acid-free paper ∞
Project Editor: Liz Smith
Designed by Matthew Tauch
Typeset in Garamond Premier Pro by Copperline
Book Services

Library of Congress Cataloging-in-Publication Data
Names: Ndaliko, Chérie Rivers, author.
Title: To be Nsala's daughter : decomposing the colonial gaze / Chérie N. Rivers.
Description: Durham : Duke University Press, 2023. | Includes bibliographical references and index.
Identifiers: LCCN 2022026526 (print)
LCCN 2022026527 (ebook)
ISBN 9781478019091 (paperback)
ISBN 9781478016458 (hardcover)
ISBN 9781478023722 (ebook)
Subjects: LCSH: Harris, Alice Seeley. | Documentary photography—Congo (Democratic Republic) | Atrocities—Congo (Democratic Republic) | Violence—Congo (Democratic Republic) | Congo (Democratic Republic)—History—To 1908. | Congo (Democratic Republic)—Politics and government—1885–1908. | BISAC: PHOTOGRAPHY / History | SOCIAL SCIENCE / Black Studies (Global)
Classification: LCC DT655 .N333 2023 (print) | LCC DT655 (ebook) | DDC 967.2/01—dc23/eng/20220804
LC record available at https://lccn.loc.gov/2022026526
LC ebook record available at https://lccn.loc.gov/2022026527

Cover art: Photograph from *Contradict: Untitled 14*. Result of the Decomposing the Colonial Gaze workshop in Lubumbashi, Democratic Republic of the Congo, 2018. Courtesy of Yole!Africa.

for the
disremembered

April, again

To my beloved children,
to my fellow wonderers,

A wise one once told me only a fool takes a proverb literally. That was the first gift.

The second was a map oriented not to space, not to time, but to process.

Together these gifts gave me a certain kind of courage — to court wisdom knowing that my light-skinned long-locked body can never afford to play the fool; to insist that despite the frequent and frenzied veneration of things, process always, always outweighs product as measure of value.

And for a time, that was enough.

But then came you, ushering in your infinite wake the maternal gift of reverent rage. And a riddle:
For to withhold these gifts (of proverb and process) is to extinguish their power and thus deprive you of your birthright. But to unleash them is a cavernous risk against which there is no guarantee.

I suppose this is why some see in every gift a curse. Indeed, to be allegiant to proverb is, to some, an invitation to be mistaken; to venerate process is, in one view, to be perpetually out of synch; to live with reverent rage is to rupture. Gift or curse, there is no guarantee.

But there is, perhaps, a hint of grace. For riddles, like proverbs, are mighty teachers. Among other things, they have the power to remind us what is at stake. And beyond the petty stakes of pride or fear of censure, what, to my mind, is at stake is the very prospect of possibility.

And here, precisely, lies the risk: there is no well-worn path to the possibilities I aspire to pursue and yet your life and being hang in the balance. And so it is that reverent rage compels me, without guarantee, to pledge allegiance to proverb, to process, and to possibility. So it is that reverent rage compels me, without guarantee, to bequeath to you a love of riddles, the knowledge that they are everywhere, and all the courage I can muster to live by the simple truth that how and why any particular wisdom came to be is infinitely more important than what anyone might try to convince you it is "about."

This practice has taught me that your birthright is not in fact a matter of gift but a matter of choice. Yours is a choice of blessing or curse, a choice of allegiance.

A choice I put, with love, in your hands.

Contents

Preface

In July 2016, a fight nearly erupted in the *Marché du peuple* in Goma (eastern Congo) over a pop-up exhibition of colonial photographs. The artists who installed the exhibition were enrolled in a workshop, Decomposing the Colonial Gaze, and wanted to see the public's reaction to the images that introduced the Congo to the Western world. Between fishmongers and mountains of used shoes, they hung pictures of slaves amassing ivory, missionaries instructing children in jungles, women and men with scarified faces. But the photograph that sparked anger was of a lone man with an imposing gaze. Art historians captioned it *Chief from Kasai*, but marketgoers questioned why a chief would be pictured without advisers and guards and, more urgently, who had the power to break cultural norms and isolate him.

Their critiques challenge scholarly interpretations of the photographs, of colonial history, and of visual representation. But they were, in effect, uttered in a vacuum—the photographer is long dead, and the scholars who study her archive are in distant institutions; thus their insights were limited to the crowds that chanced through the market. That is, until the artists decided to create new works that speak back—after more than a century—to the historic photographs.

Since then, these artists have produced a body of work that has been described as a "catalytic encounter between contemporary Congolese artists and the archive that codified the aesthetics of atrocity in the Western world."[1] In the tradition of academic critique, this is an apt description of their works, for they are actively interrupting established ways of representing and intervening in Congolese life.

But there is more to the story than that. Indeed, when pressed, these artists insist it is the process—not any product—of Decomposing the Colonial Gaze that matters most. That it was the process (not any product) that forever changed how they perceive the world, that might change how others, too, perceive. I cannot tell their stories of process; those are theirs to tell. But I can vouch for their insistence on process because I, too, was forever changed by the process of Decomposing the Colonial Gaze.

Oddly enough, it was not my role as coauthor of the Decomposing curriculum that changed me, though that was certainly illuminating. Nor was it my role as coinstructor of the early cohorts, though that was a precious privilege. No, it was not until I applied the process of Decomposing the Colonial Gaze to my own self that I was irreversibly transformed. And that did not happen until I wrote this book.

Truth be told, I set out to write, at arm's length, about the artists and their works; to play my part in the choreography of critique by "theorizing a decolonial aesthetic narrative as it unfolds" (as I proclaimed in my bid for a prestigious fellowship). But when I sat down, in earnest, to write about Decomposing the Colonial Gaze, I found myself in the grip of a grave dilemma. Because, the truth is, Decomposing is not only about learning to recognize (or critique) the colonial gaze; it is about recalibrating one's imagination in order to perceive possibilities rendered invisible by colonial logic. And for all my reverence for the choreography of critique, I am not blind to its role in sustaining colonial invisibilities.

So I chose, instead, to recalibrate my imagination. And that forever changed me. That is, in part, because reckoning with colonial invisibilities robbed me of many familiar words. Gone was my ability to write, say, about "Congo" (or anywhere else branded by nation) without invisibilizing the many other ways of knowing that particular land. Gone, too, was my ability to write about things "past" or "present" without invisibilizing the many other ways of knowing the directionality of time. Gone were so many ways of naming and claiming the "people," "places," and "things" about which my "expertise" "qualifies" me to produce "valuable" "knowledge." And gone was my ability—to say nothing of my willingness—to pretend otherwise. This last is, perhaps, the most important. For, thus destabilized in space and time, I found myself in need of new cardinal directions toward which to orient. So that is the story I wrote here—the story of my own reimagining.

Frankly, there is a certain vulnerability to publishing a record of this transformation. Yet that is precisely the urgency of this book: it is vulnerable, and, for those willing to engage the process it details, it is, potentially, transformative. As a Black woman with the privilege of sharing my perspective, my priority for this book is to aid and abet those who counterbalance the tradition of critique with equally robust emphasis on processes that enable—indeed demand—radical shifts of perception and thus of action.

So let me be explicit: this book is very much a process, not a product.

My hope is that courageous readers might engage it as a transformative, rather than an informative, text. That they might see this project not primarily as a disciplined, or disciplinable, scholarly study but an as "invitation to build a renewed imagination" (as one anonymous reader was kind—or keen—enough to suggest).

This matters to me because I have spent this lifetime in a Black body. I have spent it as a daughter, as a mother. And that has taught me, beyond the shadow of a doubt, that learning to see beyond (and beneath, and through) systems of normalized violence is prerequisite to learning to imagine—and to enact—possibilities that actually sustain life.

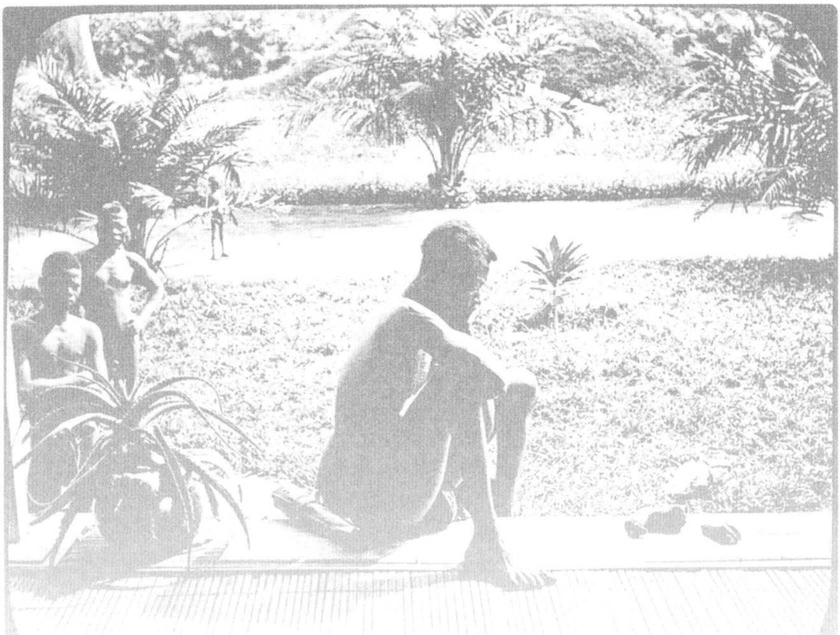

But on the other hand, it would be a great mistake to assume that the dead are absolutely powerless. They are powerless only to give the full answer to the new questions posed for the living by history. But they try! Whenever they hear the imperious cries of the people in a crisis, the dead respond.

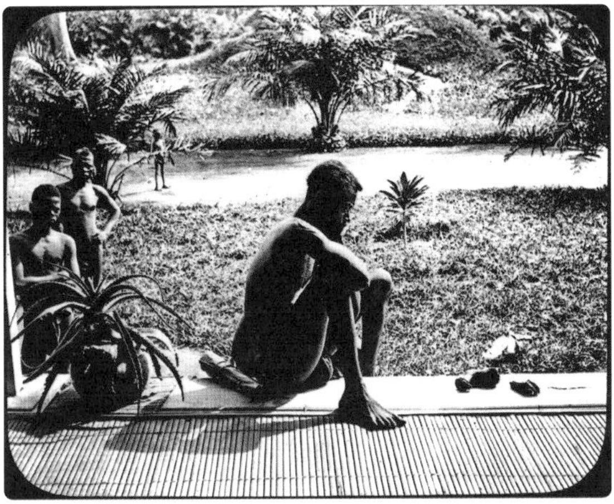

I. Elegy for Nsala

There are at least three things wrong with this picture. There is the fact of what it shows. There is the fact that it is forgotten. And there is the fact that it exists.

Each of these wrongs is haunting.

The fact of what it shows—a man they say was called Nsala gazing at the hand and foot of his five-year-old daughter, which were hacked off by police because he failed to deliver an exorbitant quota of rubber in King Léopold's Congo—haunted a British missionary named Alice Seeley Harris. So she took this photograph, that the world might see.

A dozen decades on, the fact that it—the visual evidence that buoyed the famed abolitionist campaign that overthrew Léopold's despotic regime—could be forgotten haunted researchers combatting modern slavery. So, among other things, they sent this photograph to me, that I might help remember.

And now I, too, am haunted. Not so much by what this photograph shows nor by its forgetting—by those I am alarmed and dismayed. But it is the fact that it exists that haunts me.

I look at it and wonder what the child behind the palm tree thought as it was taken. That child who watched a white woman in the heart of Congo meticulously arrange a man she called Nsala in profile to accentuate his gaze at the severed limbs of his daughter. I look at it and wonder what that child might say—if, unlike Nsala's daughter, they lived to see it—about the fallacies of a "liberation" that transferred power from the hands of a despotic man to the hands of a despotic state. I look at it and wonder how and when and where and why the lust for rubber—or anything else—is justified, how (and where and when and why) dismemberment or specious "liberation" are the only options. I look at it and wonder everything that it is possible to wonder about the world that broke Nsala and his daughter. Including how and where and when and why it might be changed. And by whom.

And so I wrote this book. As an elegy for Nsala and his daughter. And that others, too, might be haunted.

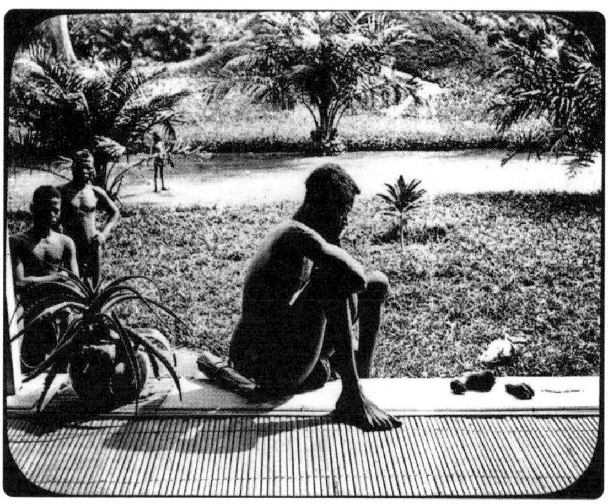

2. To See Nsala's Daughter

It's harder than it should be, seeing the dead. It took me forty years. Or maybe it took me forty years to believe my eyes, to rid this Black body of so many white lies. As hauntings will, the demand to see the dead struck at a most inopportune moment. I was leading a workshop called Decomposing the Colonial Gaze, which, this particular time, happened to take place in southern Congo. I was supposed to be the expert, to choreograph a radical encounter with history, to usher a motley band of artists, educators, and civil society leaders to the brink of revolution. When a dead girl walked in with my sons.

They were in pursuit of "Marie," a very alive seven-year-old, who entered the lecture hall quietly in search of her mother. Fresh from school, Marie kept her eyes politely downcast, her books tucked neatly in arm. But something was wrong with her forehead. I could not tell quite what—a gash of some sort, glistening with both live and crusted blood. *Perhaps she fell*, I thought, *perhaps she fell.*

No one seemed concerned. To the contrary, her wound elicited knowing nods. She was treated to a volley of fist bumps as she made her way past, to whispered jokes about the perils of school—lapses of language, the cardinal sin of curiosity, an inventory of infractions that rupture flesh. To those who knew better than I, Marie's was a familiar wound, its shape and placement a signature of reprimand, a stamp of bettering, of the schoolmaster's promiscuous lash.

It was about to dawn on me that Marie did not fall.

Instead, my very alive five-year-old trailed Marie into the lecture hall, his young brother in tow. Oblivious to her bloodied head and emboldened by her entry into the hallowed space of learning, they followed her in hopes of play. And the dead girl came, too.

Accustomed to the workings of bodies, my boys were not alarmed when they noticed the blood. No, they were not alarmed by the blood. But they curdled with fear when they noticed the conspicuous lack of concern. Still grasping at the realization that Marie did not fall, I was no help to them. And in my paralysis, I missed the fleeting chance to deflect their gaze, to distract, to distort, to do anything to keep them from the gaping abyss of the poisonous question that was blossoming on their unblemished brows: *What could possibly make Marie's wound normal in anyone's eyes?*

Their alarm at the absence of alarm tipped the scales of my vision. And that was how I learned to see the dead.

NSALA'S DAUGHTER

With my newly haunted sight (and with time) came the ravenous demand that I do better. That, like my boys and the dead girl in their wake, I gaze into the gaping abyss of Marie's ruptured forehead and see that the something that is wrong is not the wound (after all, flesh heals) but the fact that wounds—wounds gauged into bodies in the name of progress, wounds gauged into landscapes in the name of development, wounds gauged into economies in the name of freedom—that all these wounds are seen as normal in anyone's eyes, that their violence is so thoroughly sanctioned as to make itself invisible.

In a world erupting in flames, bullets, and bombs, I need not point out that the invisibility of sanctioned violence is not a uniquely Congolese problem. It just so happens that Congo is where I first learned to see the dead. But this is not a story about Congo; it is a story about how perceptions are conditioned, about the many violences that occur in plain sight, about our collective willingness to see them without seeing that they are not in fact inevitable but rather the predictable outcome of wretched choices that we willfully disguise as laws and history, as facts of time and space. It is about the painful truth that it is easier to absolve ourselves with the illusion that this-is-how-things-are (and thus that there-is-nothing-we-can-do) than it is to learn to see the dead.

What I mean by seeing the dead is looking for the possibilities rendered invisible by systems of normalized violence. This is, quite literally, a matter of seeing ghosts, of seeing what once was or could have been, what isn't but still could be. And ghosts are everywhere.

My particular ghost happens to be Nsala's daughter. She is the dead girl who haunts my vision. I do not mean the hand and foot of her remains displayed to her father for failing to meet his rubber quota in King Léopold's Congo. I do not mean the photograph of his contemplation displayed to the world to arouse righteous fury. Those are not the girl, but traces of the systems of normalized violence that render her invisible.

The problem is, so many of us are conditioned to believe our eyes in such a way that her hand and foot are all we think we see. That is what her photographer saw; that is what the masses saw, whose lugubrious outrage championed her cause, whose transcontinental heroism secured transfer of her posthumous custody from the hands of a despotic king to the hands of a despotic state. And called it moral victory.

Of course I share the horror over her dismemberment. But I no longer choose to believe my eyes. What stung me out of the complacency of outrage was the wretched answer to the unblemished question, *What could possibly make Marie's wound normal in anyone's eyes?* The answer is this: the same thing that made Nsala's daughter's wound if not normal at least circumstantial, the same thing that sends bullets and bombs through Black and brown bodies the world over in the name of security, and progress, and peace.

To many of us, none of these things are in fact normal. So we rage against them. Like Nsala's daughter's champions, we protest and counterprotest, we enact and repeal laws, we sit in and walk out. But how often do we look for the dead? How often do we venture over the brink of invisible possibility, much less take up permanent residence in what still could be?

Despite my many claims to activism, in my case the answer was not often enough. Not for lack of caring or for lack of will, but for lack of ability. Because it turns out seeing the dead is difficult. It is a matter of seeing against the grain of everything we are taught to believe, seeing not only around corners but through solid surfaces, in the dark.[1] Seeing the dead is a matter of unraveling the gilded prisons we so ruthlessly substitute for reality, the sanctuaries we desecrate in our lust for absolution.

And it comes at a cost. I, for one, lost something precious the day I first saw the dead. I lost the illusion of belonging. I may well be better off without it, but it was an excruciating loss. It was severed by my ravenous gratitude for my sons' horror on Marie's behalf, by the sickening comfort of unfamiliar violence, the naked relief that this particular wound did not—and would not—happen to them.

My relief was, of course, ridiculous. Why extol the limits of the schoolmaster's promiscuous lash amidst an epidemic of bullets sanctioned for Black bodies? In every conceivable sense my relief was ridiculous. And it was also a source of shame.

TO SEE

Shame is never pleasant, but it has a way of being productive. In my case, the shame of relief over a wound deferred forced me to see differently. It forced me to see that my battle with diasporic alienation was its own form of blindness, that rejecting one system of normalized violence in favor of another is not liberation, much less revolution, but complicity. It forced me to accept that violence, like invisibility, transcends geography, and that geography alone cannot yield belonging in the aftermath of transatlantic history.

But that is not all. Shame of relief over a wound deferred forced me to see that I was guilty of the same lethal lack of alarm I so condemned on behalf of Marie, perhaps not about the gouging of foreheads but about countless infractions I willfully seduced myself to believe are beyond my control, about countless infractions I stubbornly refused to see. It forced me to see in the gaping wounds of this whole breaking world my own part in the logic of absolution that dismembered Nsala's daughter. Because the logic has not changed with time, only acquired different trappings.

In this sense it was the shame of relief over a wound deferred that set me on the quest to see Nsala's daughter. To see her is, in part, a matter of seeing the systems of normalized violence that render her invisible, a matter of seeing the lethal elixir of markets and merchandise that fracture the world into classes of color, value, and viability and absolve murderous madness in the name of science, and law, and freedom, and faith.

But to stop there is still to see nothing but her severed hands and feet. To see the rest of her is to see the conditions that enable her to be whole. And that is an entirely different view of the world. It is one in which we recognize the chasmic difference between laws (those immutable truths of nature) and rules (those calculated choices of human beings), in which we recognize the history of perjury that conflates the latter with the former. And, in cleaving laws from rules, we not only face the fallacies of the systems that masquerade as fact (or Truth, or Reality), but actively set about existing otherwise.

To see Nsala's daughter is, for me, a meditation, a blistering practice of imagining the circumstances that keep her whole. I am not talking about flights of retrospective fantasy, but ruthless analysis of history and possibility, of time and space, of human choices, and of all that is prescribed by Reality as beyond the bounds of scrutiny. It is a futuristic discipline of seeing, in each and every encounter, the conditioning of perceptions that compels allegiance to systems of sanctioned violence that are actively destroying the very possibility of life even as we pretend there-is-nothing-we-can-do.

At best, to see Nsala's daughter is to unravel every hidden crease of our perceptions, to sever allegiance to systems of normalized violence, and thus unmoored, to take deathly seriously the question, *What if to see is not to believe but rather to create?*

3. To Decompose

My unraveling began with an email.

> Dear Dr. Rivers,
>
> Given the chance would you pass once more, in reverse, through the door of no return? If so, we have something for you.
>
> Sincerely.

That is not an exact quote. It is, rather, the message that wafted through the meticulous professionalism of a haunting correspondence. There was, of course, more to it than that.

There were niceties: *We hope this message finds you well . . . We realize this is a delicate issue, but . . . We are writing in hopes that . . . Through your connections in the Congo . . . And, in light of your impressive credentials . . . You might be willing to assist us . . .*

There was context: *We have recently come into possession of the archive of Mrs. Alice Seeley Harris, a British missionary who took a series of photographs between 1896 and 1904 that exposed the atrocities King Léopold was committing in the Congo Free State. As I trust you are aware, her photographs drove a robust international campaign in the UK and the United States that eventually pressured the Belgian government to purchase the territory from Léopold in 1908. This campaign was among the first to marry technology to humanitarian action; thus Mrs. Harris's photographs are celebrated as a founding model of humanitarian photography.*

There was also a disclaimer: *We understand that, despite their celebrated political impact, these photographs are problematic given the context of European colonialism, the "civilizing mission," and the politics of ethnographic photography/collecting.*

A note of urgency: *As part of our larger antislavery project, we are eager to solicit Congolese perspectives on and responses to these historic images. After all, Mrs. Harris's photographs were among the first to present Congo to much of the Western world. What's more, they remain a foundational model of humanitarian photography and advocacy in the West.*

A hook: *Yet, to the best of our knowledge, her photographs are not accessible in Congo, nor have Congolese audiences had occasion to comment on or critique them.*

Some technicalities: *We are in the process of digitizing some five hundred of the thousand or so photographs she took. To make them accessible. To decolonize the archive, as it were.*

And an appeal: *Should you be interested in a collaborative educational and/or creative partnership centering on these images we would look forward to working with you.*

It was all appropriately sober. And flattering. But the message was clear: please take the photographic remains of Nsala's daughter—and hundreds of her compatriots—and usher them home.

The ironies were not lost on me—the dismembered delivered into the hands of the dislocated in hopes of return. *re × turn. verb: 1. Come or go back to a place or a person. 2. Give, put, or send (something) back to a place or a person.* How does one, who does not belong, usher the remains of that which was wrongfully taken "back" to a place that no longer exists?

I received the email not so long after I had howled the first of my infinite Black boys into being, when the ferocity of care was still calcifying into habit. When offered custody of Nsala's daughter, I said yes. Without pause. In retrospect my acceptance was dictated both by the chapped and sleepless alchemy of intimacy and by the feral will that this world erupting in flames, bullets, and bombs not make of his body a replica of hers.

I expected this mission to be one of intelligent rage.[1] To enfold me in the defiant ranks of Black motherhood from whence I might find the fury to love despite the odds. I expected to labor, perhaps to crack. But I did not expect to unravel.

One rarely does.

We set out, Nsala's daughter and I, with an accomplice (I wielded the credentials, he the Congolese passport). Our first stop was the marketplace. It seemed a fitting entry, a familiar tide of bustle and barter, of pounded roots and wilted greens. With a dozen or so of her compatriots—some shackled by the neck and wrists, some carrying hammocked white men, some baring scarified bodies—we installed Nsala's daughter between fishmongers and mountains of used shoes.

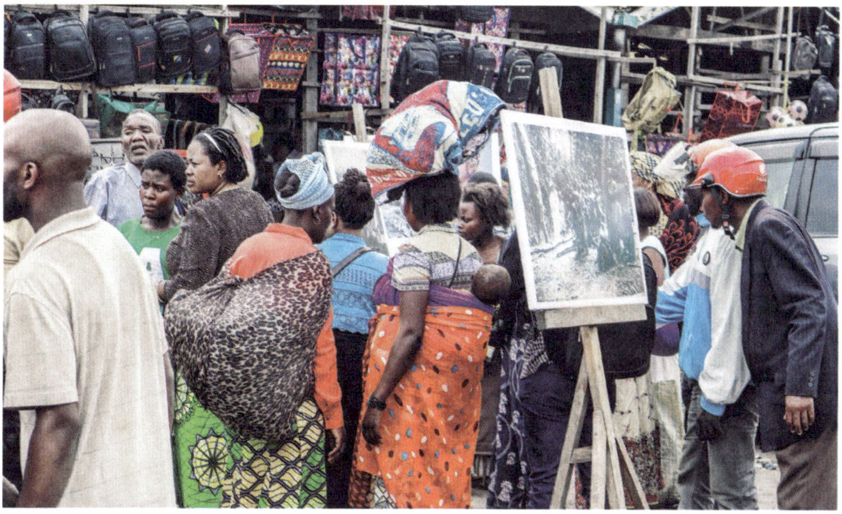

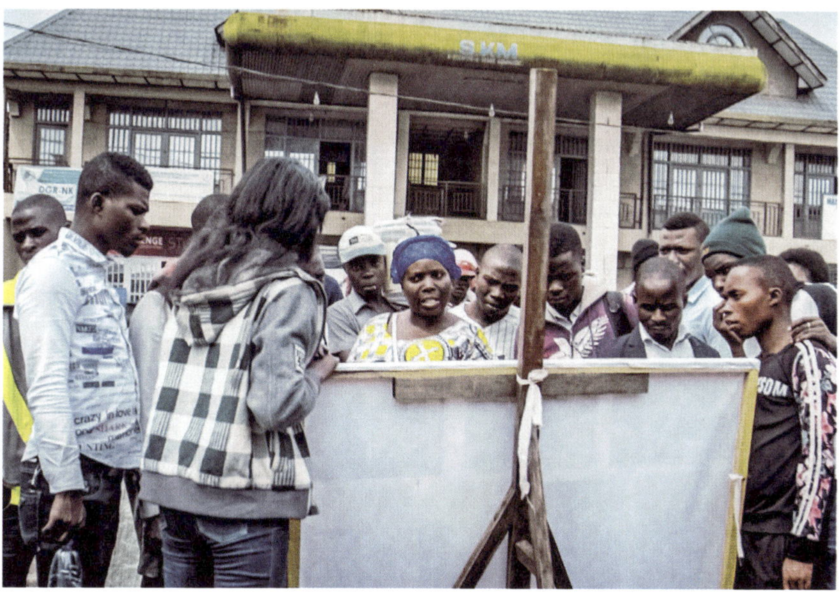

Ancestral specters among salted meat, they did not take long to provoke: a cacophony of curiosity, reproach, disagreements, one of which nearly came to blows in a battle of opinions. Is colonization to blame? Or to revere? Is initiation into the modern world a mark of progress? Or of shame? Look at the children learning to read! Look at the children learning to hate! Look at the ports, the mighty ships, the cargo! Look at the whips, the tethered bodies, the cargo!

re × turn. noun: 1. An act of coming or going back to a place or activity. 2. A profit from an investment.

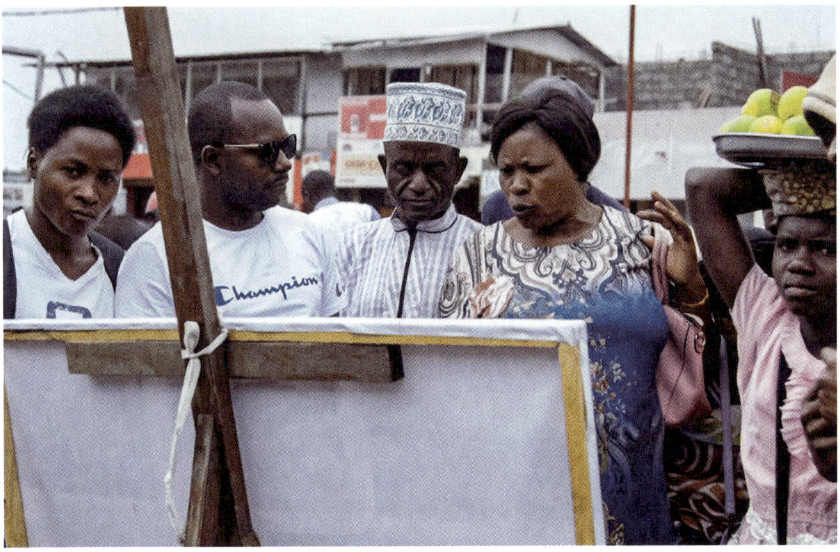

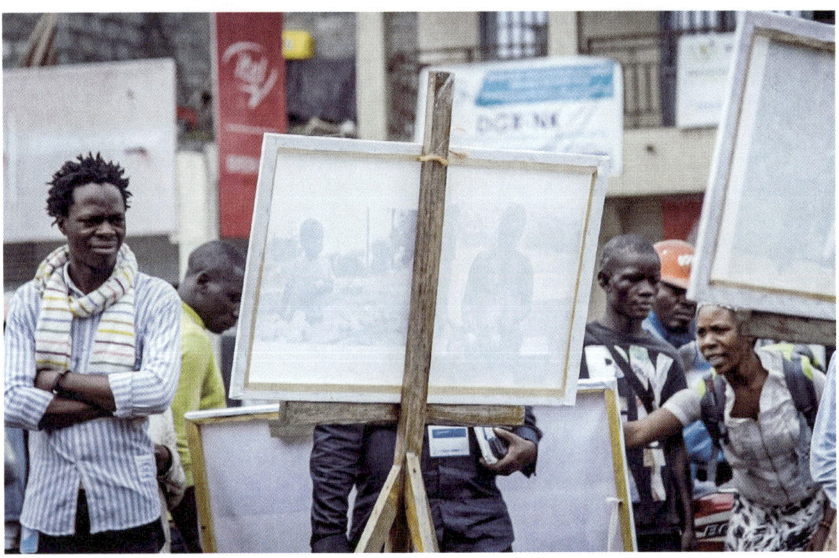

The argument raged on, trembling cold. But no one saw Nsala's daughter. They sucked their teeth in outrage over her mutilated limbs, raised blistering eyes to hallow her soul. But no one saw her. What I mean is no one *looked* for anything beyond that which her photographer had imprisoned in sepia. The gaze of a British missionary, however well intentioned, was, in effect, the final view that foreclosed any other possibility. The door of no return. The portal and the view through which Nsala's daughter, like so many beloved children of diaspora, is "disremembered and unaccounted for, she cannot be lost because no one is looking for her."[2]

No one is looking for her. I could wax poetic about regimes of sight that look right past us, right through us, that bleed us of the will, even the imagination, to know that we are lost, much less to see the world otherwise. I could rail against blind allegiance to the cult of vision suffocating the globe, leeching possibility and perspective. But the truth is I was not looking for Nsala's daughter either. Even as I cradled her remains, even as I trembled with cold fury, I was not really looking.

Better said, I did not know how to see her. I knew how to rage about her invisibility, to liken it to my own diasporic alienation. I knew who and how to blame for our mutual disremembering. But I did not know how to see beyond it.

I say all this in retrospect. At the time I would have said it differently. In the immediate aftermath of ushering Nsala's daughter through market brawls, university debates, civil society discussions, I would have—and did—diagnose a paralyzing collision with transatlantic history. And, in the spirit of *a collaborative educational and/or creative partnership centering on these images*, my accomplice and I would have—and did—propose a remedy. Propelled by the cold trembling of curating return, we conjured a process, called it a curriculum, and, unbeknownst to us, set about unraveling ourselves.

DECOMPOSING THE COLONIAL GAZE

Names are sacred. Knowing this, we christened our curriculum *Decomposing the Colonial Gaze*. Not deconstructing, and certainly not decolonizing. Decomposing.

Like other modes of reconfiguring power, decomposing is a liberatory practice. The antithesis of composing, it is a process of learning to look for the disremembered, the unaccounted for, and, by looking for them, of offering them the dignity of being lost. *And* it is a matter of meditated decay, of studied and cathartic necrosis that incubates possibility in its wake.[3]

But decomposing does not afford the arm's length of theory. And I will not write about it thus. It is a thing of bodies and of being, a feral-willed pursuit of the fury to love—and to live—despite the odds, a seismic promise to see the world anew. To see Nsala's daughter.

For all its cathartic possibility, the practice of Decomposing the Colonial Gaze hinges, first, on technical skill. It requires that we recognize the varied possibilities of what and how and why we see.

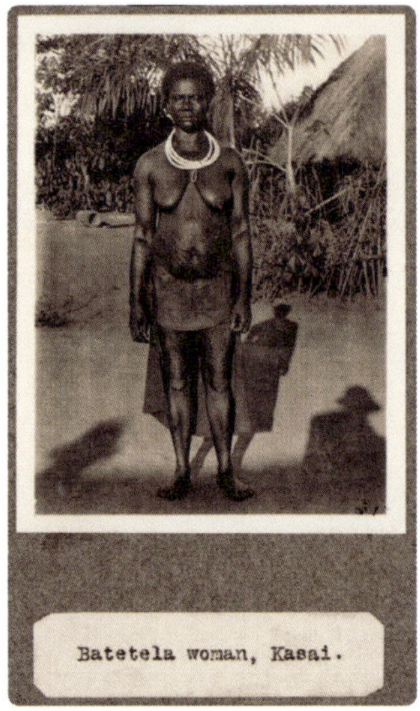

Batetela woman, Kasai.

For instance, from one point of view—that of the photographer, perhaps—this photograph depicts a native woman. Performing the grammar of equity, the camera is on par with her gaze. Neither looking up at nor down upon her, it pays her neither the complement of elevating nor the offense of diminishing her.

From this point of view we detect a meticulous study of lines: the vertical subject, well centered in a horizontal landscape, an homage to the rule of thirds. And, by their convergence on the intricacies of belly, these lines betray a scintillating curiosity. (In deference to propriety we are meant to equate this curiosity with anthropology and laud the pursuit of science.)

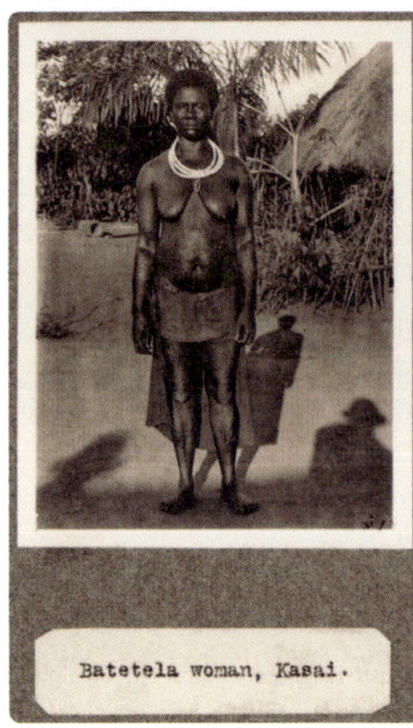

Batetela woman, Kasai.

To decompose this image further, we can pursue the question of navigation—that is, how our eyes are drawn through its maze. Snared by the dazzling brightness, we most likely enter by way of the necklace, then follow the light first up then down her body. The gravity of lines may well compel us to linger on the belly, perhaps the thighs. Then, buoyed by the necklace, to ascend, by way of her face, to the sky.

Scanning the sky we might decipher the texture of her surroundings, the geometry of leaf and light that lands our gaze on the smooth earth, from whence we continue to scan, always attuned to the necklace, whether resisting or yielding to it. If we fix our sights forcefully on the background, we have occasion to glean a wealth of information—about architecture, cooking utensils, garden plots. Thus, from one perspective, this is a photograph of "native life."

This is the what (a native woman) and the why (for the benefit of knowledge) from the photographer's point of view. The how (because she had a camera and, inherently, the right to photograph whom and how she pleased) is meant to be a given, so obvious it is invisible, simply True.

The colonial gaze: a stance and a logic of invisible power. Through it this "native woman"—like all native peoples, lands, and ways—is both exotic and inferior. She is "evidence" in the "science" of race, an object of anthropological study, a curiosity that deviates from and thus enforces the (white, Western) norm, a commodity in the logic of capital. But not a human being in her own right. Not even in the eyes of those who would "liberate" her from a despot.

But what happens if we look further, resist the pull of the necklace and the scarified belly and look at this woman's face? Hers is another gaze entirely. True, she is squinting against the afternoon sun, but there are other prompts for her hardened stare.

Indeed, she knows at least two things we are not meant to know: she knows that her isolation in this photograph is both fiction and infraction. We can see this if we look properly. We can see, from the long draping back of her skirt, that she is nobility. And nobles are never meant to be pictured alone. That is the infraction.

We can also see that she is not in fact alone, that she is menaced by colonial officers whose capped shadows flank the photographer and her camera. From this perspective, this is not a photograph of a native woman but a photograph of power, a record of domination that distorts as much as it documents.

Indeed, from this perspective, the what (violence), the why (power), and the how (force)—like the invisibility they secure—are entirely different.

The colonial gaze.

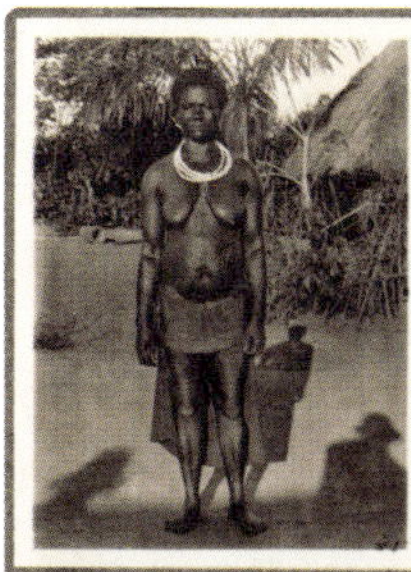

Batetela woman, Kasai.

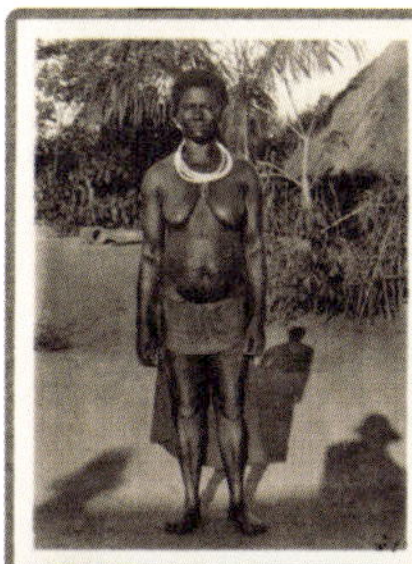

Batetela woman, Kasai.

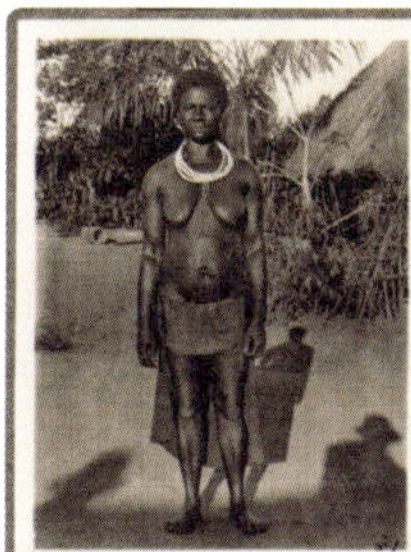

Batetela woman, Kasai.

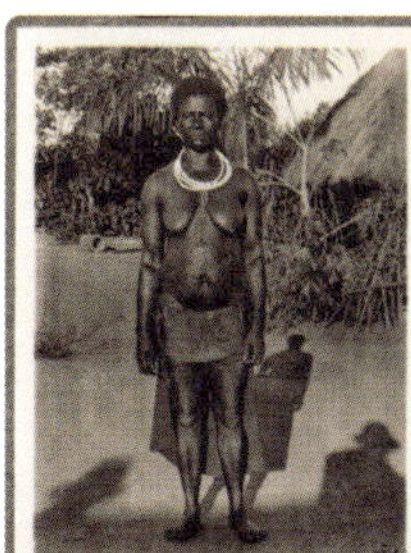

Batetela woman, Kasai.

These are the mechanics of disremembering: the sleight of hand that exalts science and power at the expense of everything else, that coerces fiction into fact in the name of Truth. This, too, is the currency of looking. If we yield to the illusion that this image is of a native woman, we will not wonder why the upturned pestle is abandoned in plain sight, why no children peer through the fence, why the queen has lost her attendants. We will not wonder where they have all gone, or under what circumstances, or whether and how they might return. If we yield to the illusion, the inhabitants of this town will not be lost because we will not look for them. We will simply see the world as if they do not exist. And they, disremembered and unaccounted for, will cease to be.

The point of Decomposing the Colonial Gaze is to return to us the possibility and the ambition of seeking that which is lost. We call it a curriculum because it is a process we curate, sometimes in workshops or courses, seminars or trainings. But it does not always take that form. Just as often it is a singular meditation, perhaps a dialogue, sometimes a sudden flash of knowing.

The constant, regardless of format, is that Decomposing the Colonial Gaze is a practice that hones our skills of sight, traces power through lines and light, through depth and shadow; a practice that fosters the persistent deployment of curiosity, the reflexes to question proximity and omission, to digest contradictory truths, to see the world anew.

These are the mechanics of unraveling the monolithic illusions of transatlantic history, the logistics of decomposing the accumulated logic of our own invisibility. And, like any vital process, decomposing the colonial gaze unfolds in stages.

REPLICATE

As anyone who has unraveled knows, the process begins not from without but from within. It is a matter, first and foremost, of knowing one's enemies. To be clear, in the practice of decomposing the colonial gaze, enemies are not nouns—not people, places, or things, not even moments or laws—but habits of perception. Those conditionings that lurk behind our eyes and discipline our vision.

In the colonial gaze, habits of perception, like everything else, are subject to the hubris of Truth imposed by false idols. These idols are many and lethal. And there is no hierarchy in the suffering they inflict, no greater or lesser evil.

For reasons of visibility we begin with the false idol of whiteness. To be seen in this bucolic scene, for example, is literally a matter of proximity to whiteness—a feature not only of the central matriarch and her shadow, but shared, too, by the planks of the bridge, the lush foliage, and, to a lesser degree, by the three "natives" near enough to reflect her glow. And while it is perhaps a stretch to suggest their forward march across a bridge (however "crude") is a metaphor of progress, there is no doubt that their two compatriots, distanced as they are from whiteness, appear as fixed and anonymous features of the natural landscape.

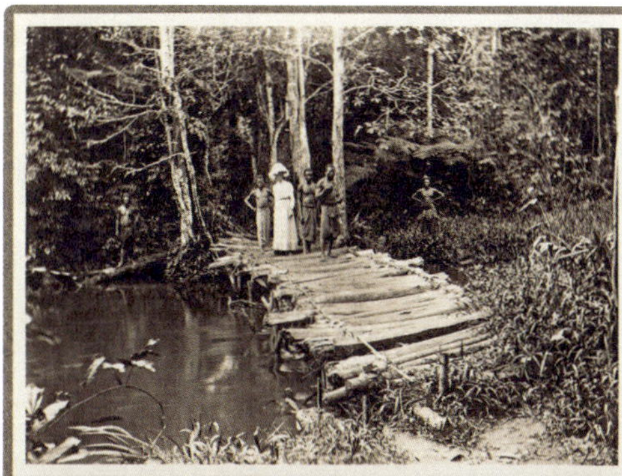

Crossing a stream near the Sankuru.

Here, too, it is whiteness that dictates our course through the image. Whether we decompose this photograph with lines or with light, it is only at the end (if at all) that we arrive on the lone "native," whose distance from the radiant white of paper and gown imprisons him in shadow.

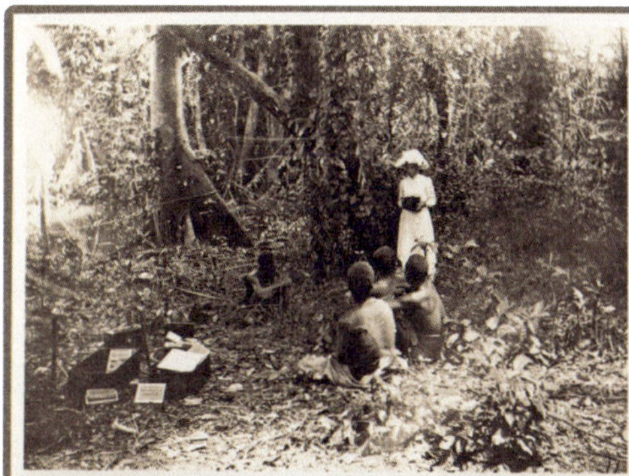

Native sitters - on the banks of the Kasai.

Of course this is, in part, a technical issue. It has much to do with the angle of the sun. And cameras—whether in the hands of missionaries, anthropologists, or their humanitarian, scientific progeny—must be calibrated to *something* in order to regulate light. They must be given a base from which to recognize all other tones. And then, as now, that something, the base against which all else is measured, is white. This so-called white balance is tradition, it is standard, it is simply how things are done. But it is not a given; it is a choice. A choice that renders white skin with intimate nuance, white faces with depth of emotion, white bodies with detail and context—with more than eyeballs and teeth. It is a choice. And this choice, as old as the art and science of photography itself, is the mechanical warden of entrenched habits of perception, and mechanical warden of the illusion that they are true.

To throw the force of habit into stark relief—to know our enemies, as it were—we set ourselves the task of replicating the colonial gaze. That is, of seeing, *on purpose*, through the lens and the logic of domination. Seeing thus causes most of us pain. But the pain stems less from the violence inherent in this way of looking than from the disarming realization that this view of the world, and of ourselves, is utterly familiar, that with or without our consciousness or our consent, we have internalized the colonial gaze.

To replicate the colonial gaze is, in part, to see just how calibrated we are to whiteness. But whiteness is not the only invisible warden of the enemy within, for the logic of domination does not manifest exclusively in color. Thus replication is also a matter of learning to see other false wardens—value, for instance—that eliminate every possibility but slavery, that, if unfulfilled, eliminate the hands and feet (to say nothing of the hearts and minds) of children.

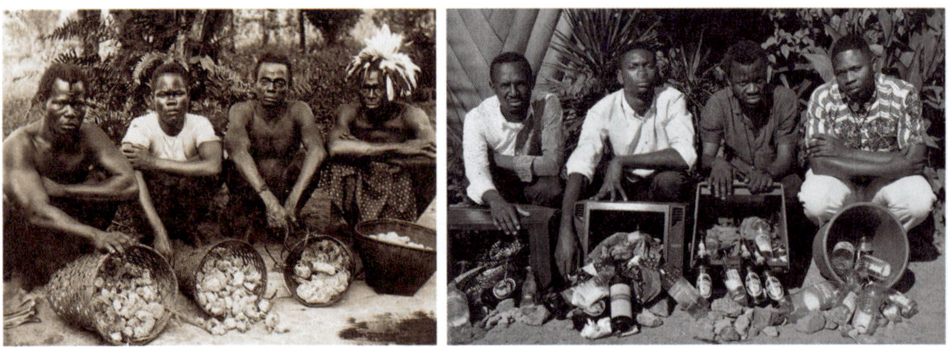

Replicate: Untitled 6

Of course, like whiteness, value is meant to be invisible, so obvious it is simply True. That was, for one, the revelation of decomposing this particular image, of replicating value past with value present. In retrospect they said,

> Decomposing this photograph shocked me because I realized I see myself in it. Not in the people, but in their wares—in the rubber, in the garbage. In everything disposable that is nonetheless more precious than human beings. When I see this photograph I understand, perhaps for the first time, how I appear in the eyes of my family. They see me through the colonial gaze, as the colonizers saw—and still see—them. As disposable. They are so desperate to prove their loyalty to Western values that they never saw me as a child but only as a symbol of the unfulfilled quota of my parents' marriage, whose divorce cast me as one whose mutilation—by ostracism, humiliation, and worse—was a measure of their proud Christian civility.

> Seeing this photograph, seeing myself, through the colonial gaze shocks me not because it is any surprise that my family despises me for reasons beyond my control, but because I have never seen myself any other way.

I have never seen myself any other way. That is precisely the shock, the collision with the prison of perception. To decompose the colonial gaze is to seize on this rupture not with pity but with the feral will to unravel.

I, for one, push this point with my body. With a simple question I make of myself, my light-skinned, long-locked self, a rupture: *When you look at me, what do you see?* Despite my vow that it is not a trick question, no one ever wants to answer, whether for fear of causing offense or distaste for stating the obvious. But when they come, as they always do with time, the answers corroborate the colonial gaze with telling precision. After preambles about looking like a "nice lady" or a "professor," someone inevitably stumbles on the prison of pigment. And the answers are always, always the same:

> In South African eyes I am—*obviously*—colored.
> In Central African eyes I am—*obviously*—muzungu.
> In West African eyes I am—*obviously*—tubaab, obroni.
> In Brazilian eyes I am—*obviously*—mulatta.
> In European eyes I am—*obviously*—foreign.
> In the eyes of the United States, depending on the makeup of my audience, I am either—and *obviously*—Black *or* a "beautiful confident woman" (a sacrifice, that is, to the liberal idol of colorblind whiteness).

Each of these things means something in the eyes of its beholder. And each, in turn, dictates possibility. To be colored or mulatta is to be wedged between, twice condemned by privilege granted and privilege withheld; to be muzungu, tubaab, obroni is to be the target of unearned respect (and of secret hopes of advantage); to be foreign is to be a problem; to be Black, in light skin, is suspect.

These categories, the afterbirth of color and value, have calcified into Truth and seeped into codes of being. And though I violate these codes religiously (at times by will, at times by ignorance), my transgression does nothing to disrupt the choreography of power.

The point, here, is less the details than the fact that, in the most literal sense, history conditions how we see, dictates how we believe our eyes. No matter how I see myself, as my light-skinned, long-locked body moves through space I assume the contours of accumulated habits of perception.

Pushing this point with my body was supposed to be a matter of pedagogy. Of opening other people's eyes to the prison of perception. What I failed to anticipate were my own aftershocks from being seen—and named—through the colonial gaze. Better said, of consciously seeing myself thus. Of realizing that I am nothing but a reflection, that it does not matter *how* I see myself, because I am imprisoned by the contortions of history.

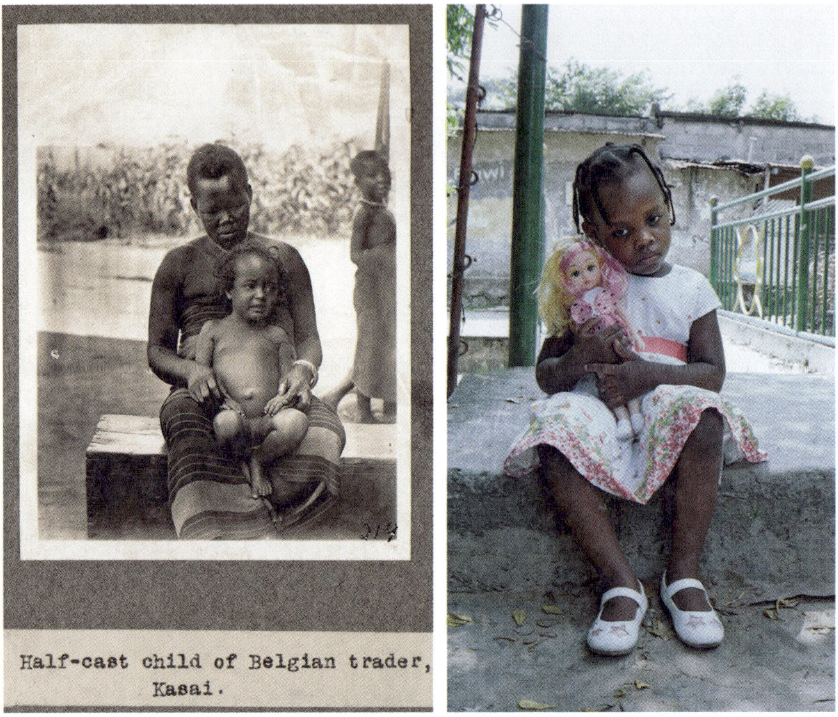

Replicate: Mirror

CONTRADICT

Just as oppression breeds resistance, the act of replicating the colonial gaze triggers the reflex to contradict it. To contradict this habit of perception is to yield to the desire to avenge the many fictions and infractions that imprison us in colonial logic. And, however many decades deferred, to demand the dignity of being lost.

Sometimes this is a matter of restoring stolen agency. As with this chief and this warrior, who, like the queen and her necklace, were falsely imprisoned; who, like the queen and her necklace, could only be severed from advisers and guards, who could only be pictured alone—be pictured at all—by force of force. To avenge these infractions is, in part, a matter of will, of granting to the motorman and the model their fervent request to be seen, and seen on their own terms.

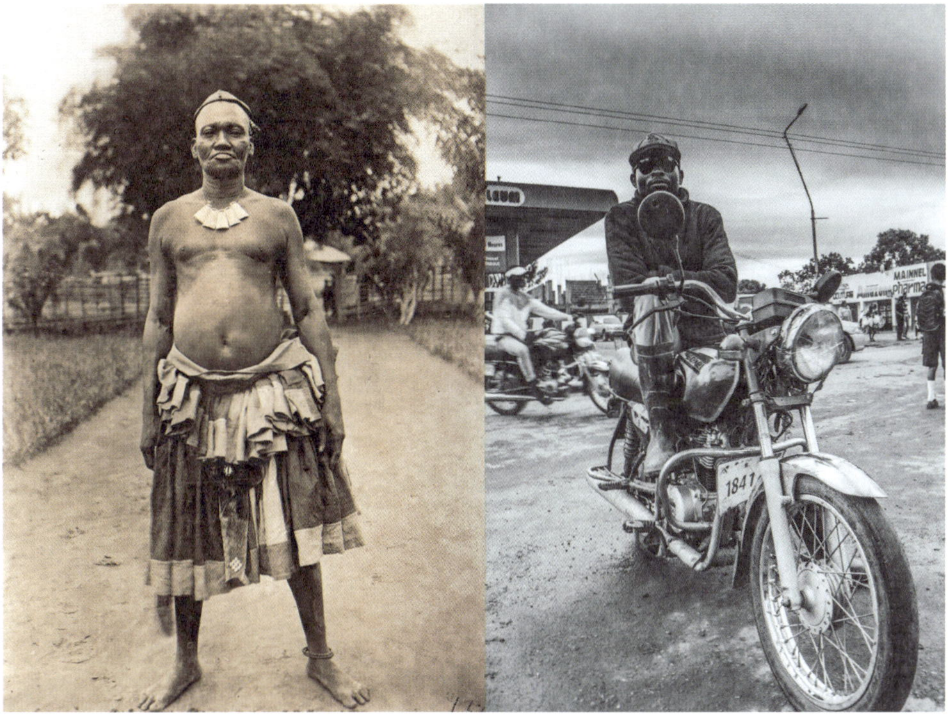

Contradict: Alone

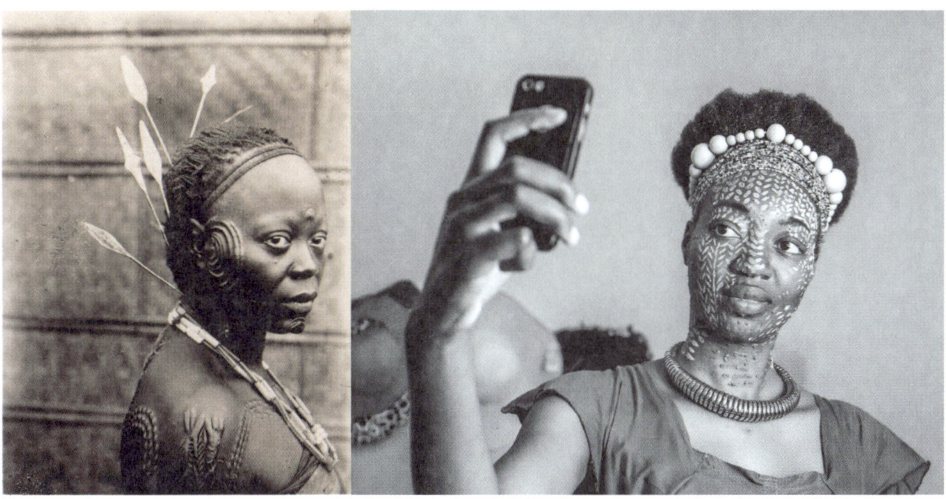

Contradict: Untitled 14

These are the dazzling, electric contradictions that make us giddy with the premonition of redemption. The bold demands for dignity that cajole us to imagine the possibility not only of being lost, but of, someday, being found.

But contradicting also provokes a more treacherous unraveling, propelled not by the heady joy of flexing rage but by a sudden crumbling. Such was the case for one whose vision was so fervently conditioned by the colonial gaze that replication had little effect. Unmoved by the vitriol colonial violences provoke in others, they sustained steadfast allegiance to the myth of altruism, to the necessity, philanthropy, even divinity of any measure taken to lift savages out of darkness. Against every accusation—of plunder, murder, and rape, of theft, extermination, and pollution—they had an invincible refrain: *education, they brought us education!*

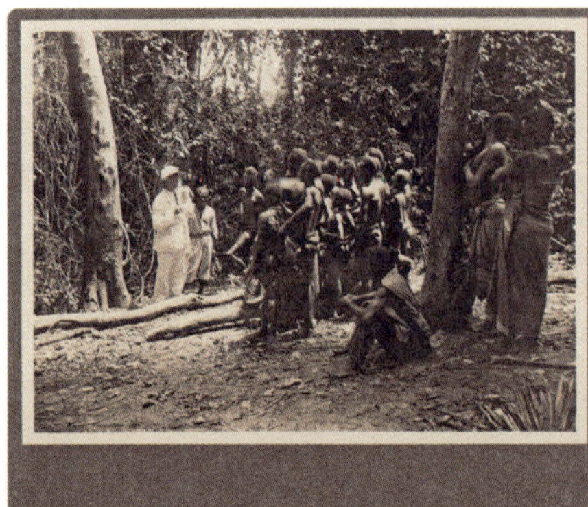

Mr. Harris shewing portrait of the late Lord Monkswell to Kasai natives.

Determined to defend the immaculate virtue of the gift of education, they set out not to contradict the colonial gaze, but to disabuse its critics of their heresy. They began with words, a passionate soliloquy to enlightenment ideals. But, arriving at a finer point about inalienability, stumbled on the language, the French that supplanted, but not fully, the nuances of mother tongue, each eroding, corroding, one another into a melee of tongue-tied mediocrity. They winced when people chuckled at an accidental pun unleashed by a rogue pronoun. They winced, but stayed the course: *they brought us education!*

Doggedly they stayed the course. Against every accusation. Until, to prove the point, they ventured into a school. Or at least they tried. Camera in hand, permissions granted, they set out to photograph the virtue of education. But as they approached the school itself, enlightenment ideals dissipated in the cold trembling of memory—of beatings (for failure of French), of humiliation (for failure of fees), of suffering (for failure of whiteness), of failure (for the fact of Blackness)—memories of mother tongues discarded, of beliefs expelled, of beings despised.[4] Of being despised.

As they would later tell us, that was the moment of sudden crumbling. Standing on the brink of a school compound, with one foot in and one foot out, seeing, for the first time, that they are collateral in the irreconcilable collision between the notion and the fact of "education." Thus destabilized, and fearing further crumbling, they persevered, plunging into the compound in hopes of salvaging the refrain, of overriding memory with the force of evidence. Of Truth.

The Truth awaiting, on that particular day in that particular school, was a young woman, shamed for arriving late, left outside to clean the walk while her agemates "bettered" their minds. No question from the schoolmaster of why she was late (because of a death), or what sacrifice her family shouldered to send her to school. Just punishment, doled out in the name of justice for breaking the hallowed rules. Just as the beatings are doled out for accidents of mother tongue, for the impertinence of curiosity, for being.

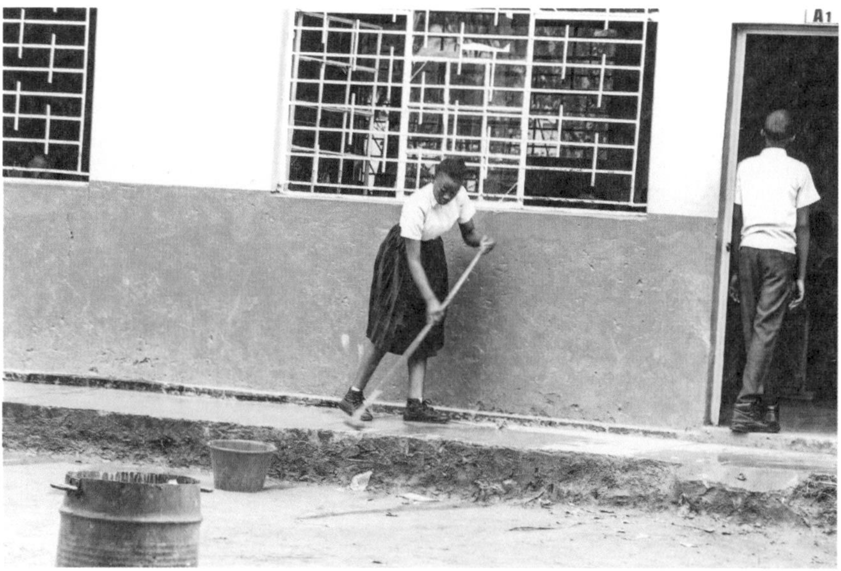

Contradict: Untitled 9.

To contradict the colonial gaze, in this instance, is to question. Who hallows the rules? Which rules? And what becomes of everything else? What does allegiance to myths of altruism discipline out of our capacity to wonder? And where does all that orphaned wondering go?

Herein lie the limits of contradiction. For all the heady joys of flexing rage, contradiction, like replication, is a symptom of impotence. Beneath its giddy premonitions of redemption, contradiction, too, imprisons perception within bars gilded not of unconscious imitation but of the promiscuous illusion—and performance—of dissent.

The point, then, of contradicting, is not just to demand the dignity of being lost, but to confront the obstacles to being sought. It is a choreographed collision with the simple fact that contradiction still gives primacy to the colonial gaze, that even to resist is to calibrate our capacity of sight to terms dictated by oppression. Rather than fanning flames of protest, to contradict is, at best, a sobering antidote to false freedoms.

And, like so many ghosts, it comes at a cost. Unraveling the promiscuous illusion of dissent requires we divest of the currency of "critique," that haughty swagger of criticism that conflates the ability to diagnose with the feral will to see—much less create—the world anew. It requires we sacrifice the fortifying slogans of sanctioned outrage, the superficial thrusts and parries against a system to which we in fact enact no alternative. It requires we unroot the complicity of congratulations and simmer in the perfect incommensurability of colonial redemption by metaphor.

Unraveling the promiscuous illusion of dissent also requires disciplined attention to detail. Not just to lines that cut through light and shadow, but lines that cut through space and time. And bodies. Because, as anyone who is paying attention knows, transatlantic dismemberment, like colonial violence, is not a thing of the past.

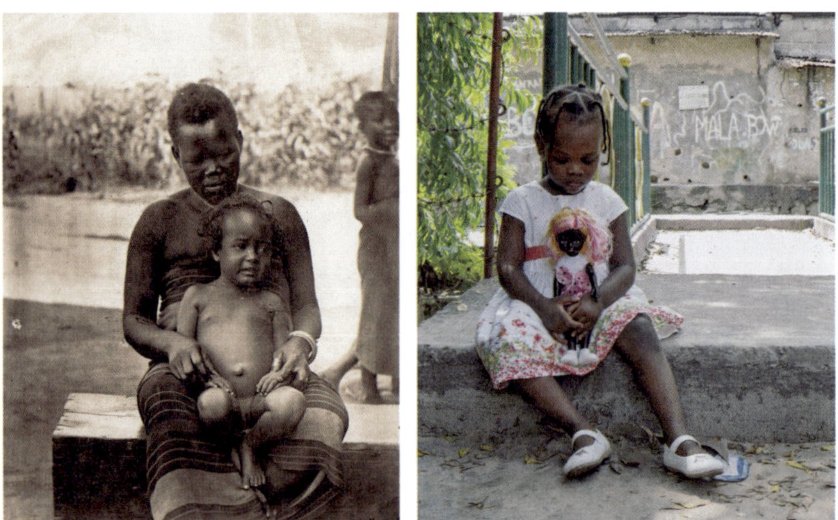

Contradi
Mirror

The point of Decomposing the Colonial Gaze is to return to us the possibility and the ambition of seeking that which is lost. Not the material, but the disremembered, the capacity to imagine. Among the lost are possibilities of perception, and also perceptions of the gilded bars—of mimicry and dissent—that keep us imprisoned without our consciousness or our consent. That is why we prescribe ourselves the discipline to replicate and contradict, to confront and oppose our enemies, to crumble and to flex our rage.

But these disciplines alone restore to us neither the possibility nor the ambition of seeking that which is lost. Instead, they expose the mechanics of disremembering, the spectrum (from mimicry to dissent) that secures allegiance to the colonial gaze. In truth, learning to replicate and contradict leaves the feral-willed among us "unable to decide whether the veil is really being lifted or lowered more firmly in place; whether [we are] witnessing a revelation or a more efficient blinding."[5]

And so we set ourselves a final task: to create. To see, that is, with pointed awareness of the habit to replicate and the reflex to contradict yet to yield to neither.

Seeing thus, like unraveling, begins not from without but from within. But it quickly becomes unruly. It quickly becomes a matter of tracing power beyond light and lines and into the contours of each daily breath. Of perceiving, in our encounters, the invisible strangleholds that dictate our possibilities of being. And, with feral will, ceasing to play our part.

Like replication and contradiction, creation, too, leaves images in its wake. Images of ghosts, of the invisible. Of imprisonment for the cardinal offense of Black hands wielding camera,

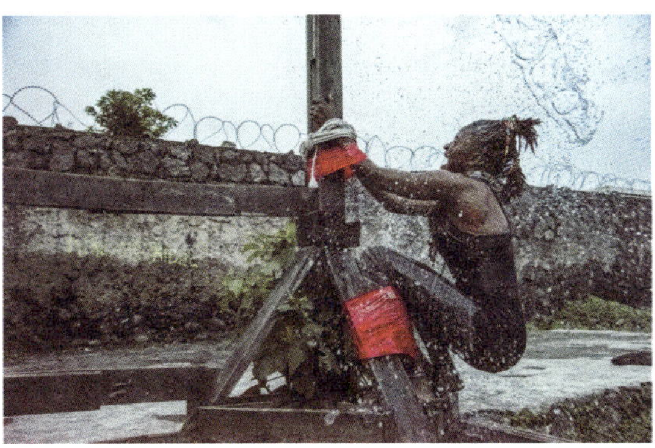

Provisional Liberty

of being migrant—never expat,

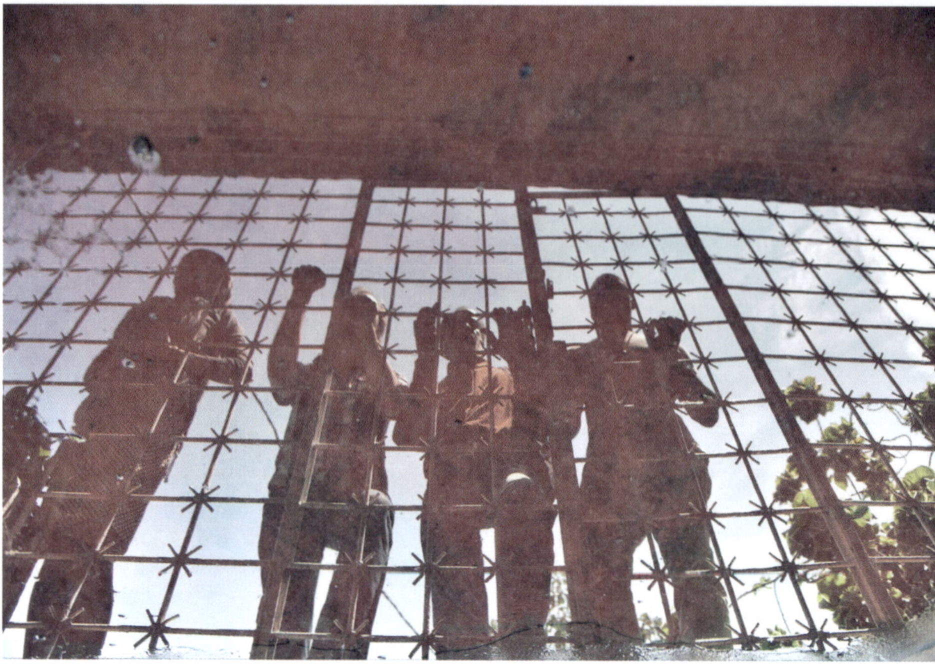

of confronting colonial logic from its underbelly,

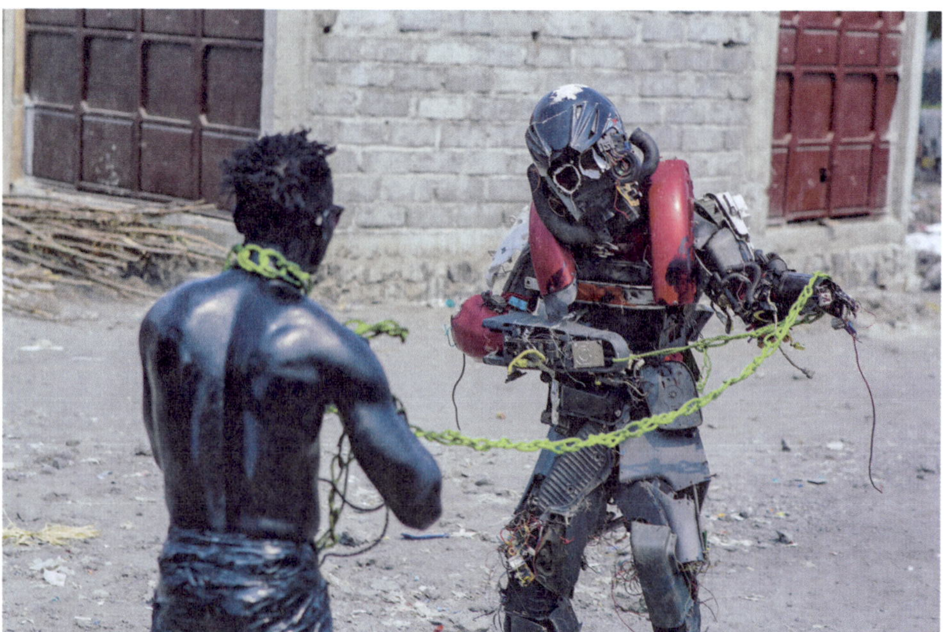

But to create is to leave more than images in one's wake. It is to see the colonial gaze at work where we least expect it—in our mothering, for instance, or our ability to enact care, in every measure of our fury to love, and live, despite the violently decreasing odds. Indeed to create is to see in the alchemy of intimacy the precious place of rage, to see in rage the precious possibility of birth.

Seeing thus unravels. It brought me, for one, to the brink of the door of no return, to the gaping abyss in which I first caught sight of the dead. So I started on a quest to seek for my infinite Black boys that which was lost. With the feral will and fervent prayer that this big breaking world not make of their memory a replica of mine.

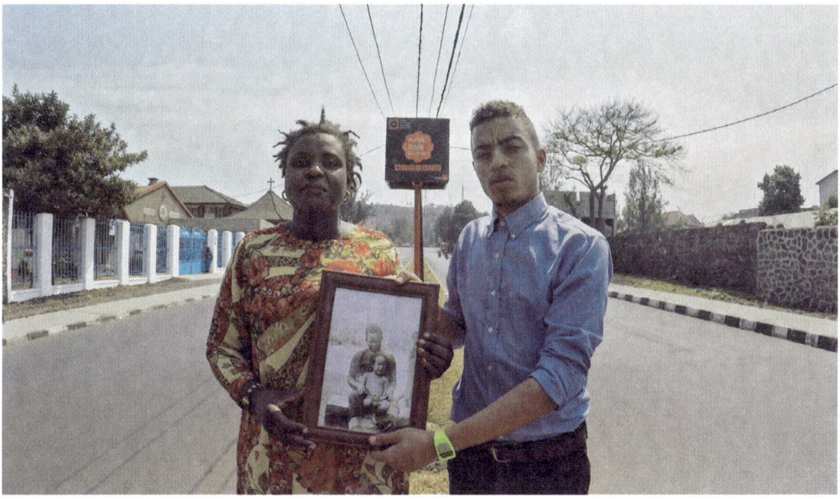

(opposite, top) At the Border

(opposite, bottom) Remains

(above) Time

4. To Replicate

It is one thing to decompose the colonial gaze in the context of a workshop. It is another thing entirely to decompose one's way through life, to confront the conditions that shape our perceptions not just in archival photographs, but in the pernicious coagulation of Reality. In principle, this is a matter of applying the reflexes of replication, contradiction, and creation to each and every breath. In practice, it perpetrates another register of unraveling because the colonial gaze not only corrodes how we see (or do not see) ourselves in images, it also perverts how we see (or do not see) ourselves in space and time.

Take, for instance, the deceptively simple question, *Where are you from?*

No matter whether its intent is innocent, this question undoes me every time. It is not as though I do not know to expect it; it is that I do not know how to answer it. Convention dictates that I should, in response, announce my place of birth and be done with it. Or sketch vignettes of a nomadic childhood, citing formative stops along the way. Or maybe conjure an immigrant ancestor to explain my idiosyncrasies. That is, one way or another I should tether myself to space in ways that make me legible.

But this has always felt to me like a trap. Like an inducement to enslave myself to a certain kind of time and a certain kind of space and thus imprison myself in the geography of the asker's imagination. In deference to civility I have, over time, concocted more or less satisfying answers—*From the belly of a slave ship by way of a capitalist state* or *From my father's womb*—but none of them ease the sting of the question nor the trembling cold anger it unleashes in me. And rarely do they satisfy the asker, who probes, undeterred, *But where are you from?*

In the aftermath of transatlantic history this is a haunted question. It is a reminder that places, like people, have ghosts. But I did not fully comprehend this until I learned to see the dead. No, as a woman of African descent, I always thought my aversion to this question was personal. Not that I was alone (much less unique), but that the source of my trembling cold anger was rooted in my biography. And my biology. That my paralysis in the face of a simple, factual question was proof of a problem that, despite being beyond my control, was with me.

And to a certain extent it is. For, like so many children of diaspora, I am perpetually haunted by the need to somehow explain that where my birth certificate says I am "from" has nothing to do with my point of origin. Even if I cannot, with any certainty, claim a specific point of origin either.

Where *am* I from? It is never an innocent question. No matter the intent, it is always a question of double consciousness.[1] It points, with cruel insistence, to the gaping "rift between the location of residence and the location of belonging" that so many of us straddle against our will.[2] And it makes a mockery of both, calls into question the very possibility of residing and belonging as simultaneous acts.

As fate would have it, I married a man who could, with a word, tie his origins to place and thus proclaim his "from" and his "roots" in one fell swoop. This, to me, bordered on the miraculous and, in my covetous imagination, dispelled the mystery of diasporic longing with precise and tangible geography, with certainty no DNA test can yield: a village called Masereka! A place with language, memory, unmutilated family trees. A place to both reside *and* belong, from which to be. I saw him as possessing that rarest and most precious of things: a from.

Imagine my shock to learn that the question undoes him, too. For all his power to point to the precise piece of earth that he calls home, the precise roots of the culture that shaped his view of the world, the best reply he can muster is, *I travel with a Congolese passport*. And even that leaves him dismayed.

The problem for him is not one of identity. Or, at least, not personal identity. He knows exactly where he is from in both biographic and biological terms. The problem is that to explain his origins in relation to a modern political map is to accept a specific construction of space and time that imprisons him in the geography of global power.

This creates, for him, a different sort of double consciousness. Though not rooted in the politics of a nation born of race, he is plagued, nonetheless, by "two-ness... two thoughts, two unreconciled strivings, two warring ideals"—not, in his case, bound "in one dark body," but, rather, in one lush land. For him, to proclaim himself "Congolese" is to define his home as it is seen "through the eyes of others, [to] measure [his] soul by the tape of a world that looks on in amused contempt and pity."[3] So he refuses. And is, like me, often at a loss for words.

I do not revel in the fact that he, too, is undone by a simple, factual question. But it has taught me something. Like mine, his problem is one of time and space. And it gives rise to trembling cold anger. But his is not personal. No, his disorientation is not rooted in body. Instead, the double consciousness I hold so deep in flesh and bone is, for him, inscribed in earth. It is a two-ness of place, seared and then congealed into the story of those who stayed, those who were not catapulted into diasporic disorientation, but who were—and are—no less dislocated in the aftermath of transatlantic history.

Learning to see our mutual disorientation perpetrated another rupture in my vision, another demand to see ghosts. Like the bloody gash in Marie's forehead, it spurred my quest to seek for my infinite Black boys that which was lost; forced me to recognize that no matter how mighty their fortress of language, names, and culture, they, like me, cannot afford the illusion of belonging. For with that illusion comes the insidious and pervasive demand to replicate colonial logic. And, in colonial logic, they, like Nsala's daughter, are disposable. In colonial logic, they are peremptorily divided against themselves—against their bodies, against their land—condemned to the exponential double consciousness of those who left *and* those who stayed.

I have learned, with time, that no amount of love or fury can immunize against the question of origin. But I have also learned that the question of origin cannot be confined to geography, that it is also a matter of stories. And there is a certain invincibility to stories. They are far from bulletproof, but stories have an uncanny power to reconfigure how we see (or do not see) ourselves in space and time, an uncanny power to help us see the dead.

I witnessed a fight once between two men, one Belgian, the other Nande. After a long day's travel through Kivu, we were sitting beside the lake, trying to shake off the remnants of our many jarring encounters with border patrols along the road. Aiming to talk about something completely different, to pay what he thought to be a compliment, the Belgian began, "The thing about you Congolese . . ."

And that was all it took.

The Nande erupted, adamant:

I am *not* Congolese.

But you *were* born in Congo, no?

No! I was born in Zaire.

Sure, but Zaire is now Congo, so . . .

This "Congo" you insist on did not exist when I was born. There was no Congo to be from. How can I be *from* a place that did not exist when I was born in it?

But you can't still say you're from Zaire? it's finished.

Finished how? Are you telling me I am from a place that does not exist?

I'm just talking about politics.

The kind of politics that make me not exist.

Don't make this personal. I mean the kind of politics that make nations change their names.

The problem is not about nations changing their names; the problem is that we ended up with nations in the first place. Whose idea was that? Not ours. So why should we be expected to use nations to explain ourselves as if they are the source of our identity? Just so we can exist in the eyes of those who chopped us up into nations in the first place? I'm sorry, my friend, but this is about as personal as it gets.

OK, so if I can't call you Congolese, what should I call you?

This is how the question of origin undoes those who stayed. It is not their inability to point to a place to claim; it is their inability to claim the place they already are. At least to claim it on their own terms. Because those terms have been buried under the slow accumulation of a certain kind of logic that now substitutes for reality.

But, instead of ceding the point, on this particular day this particular Nande decided to tell a story. It went more or less like this:

> I grew up with my great-grandmother, who lived to be 119 or thereabouts. By virtue of her age and her keen mind, she was known as a memory keeper. And among the memories she kept was the story of the day the Belgians arrived in this place. She remembered how they smelled (strange, not in a particularly pleasant way) and how that smell announced them long before they announced themselves. She remembered that when these fragrant strangers first proclaimed this territory "Congo" the people laughed and told the strangers they were lost, that Kongo was a kingdom far to the west, that this was Yira land.
>
> Of course she remembered, too, how Yira land, like all the other lands, became Congo. First with guns and whips and chains, then with laws and maps, then with constitutions and passports. She remembered when it became the fashion—or was it the law?—to hang the trilogy, in portraits, in one's house. Not the Christian trilogy, but the political trilogy of Congo.
>
> I remember this, too. As a child I was accustomed, in any respectable house, to encounter looming tributes to João, ruler of the Kongo Kingdom, whose embrace of Portuguese Catholicism in 1491 whet Europe's appetite for the heart of Africa. Next to João was Belgian king Léopold II, who, some four decades later, devoured the heart of Africa whole and belched out this place called Congo. The third face in the trilogy was mutable. In my youth it was Mobutu, but he has since been replaced by subsequent figureheads of state.

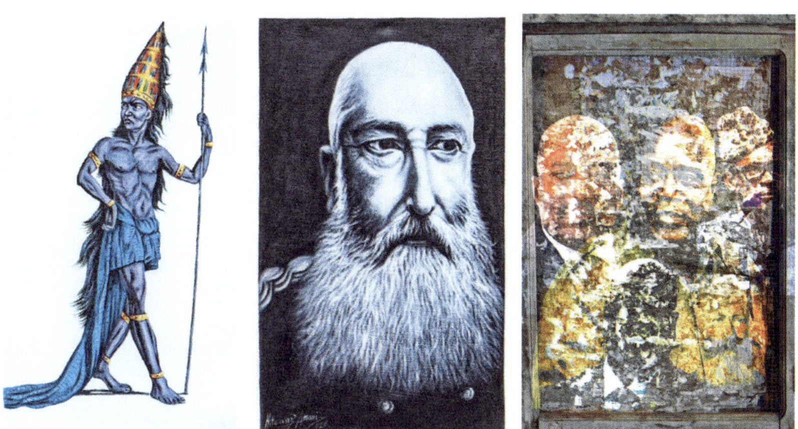

(left) João

(center) Léopold

(right) Heads of State

These were the founding fathers I encountered as a boy—the Kongo king from whom our name was plucked, the Belgian king whose misenunciation of that name christened us a nation, the heads of state who peddle that nation to the world.

But my great-grandmother made of this trilogy a quartet by adding, on an adjacent wall, a popular painting called *Ina Kale*—which translates roughly to "everything is blocked," or "no way out." It depicts the story of a man who, having set about cutting down a tree by the riverbank, finds himself menaced by a lion. To escape the lion he prepares to leap into the river, but sees the gaping jaws of a crocodile. So he begins to climb the tree, only to discover a poisonous serpent, disturbed by his chopping, slithering down the trunk. That is where the painting imprisons him—menaced by lion, crocodile, and snake, teetering on the limbs of a half-hewn tree.

The puzzle of *Ina Kale* plagued me deeply as a boy. Did the woodcutter find his way out? Was there a hidden solution I could not see? Or was he simply doomed? But, also, why did my great-grandmother add his conundrum to the wall of founding fathers? Was the impossibility of his dilemma a comment on our state? Was this her response, however many decades deferred, to the strangers who proclaimed her homeland "Congo," in whose faces she had learned better than to laugh but to whom she could nonetheless prescribe a parable?

The truth is, traveling through Kivu with you today, I felt like the woodcutter—menaced by border patrols, soldiers, and roadside checkpoints, teetering on the brink of a half-hewn state. It is a precarious sensation, though not without its ironies. To be here, in Yira land, performing rites of jurisdiction to a Congolese state, producing, again and again, passports and identity cards, to be stamped with each passage, as if enough ink or repetition can settle, once and for all, a centuries-old dispute.

"This Congo of theirs," my great-grandmother was known to say, "is nothing more than a big jagged line! It never existed until someone set about drawing it." She defied the line as she could. But to her dying day she pondered what kind of line has such power to draw a people and a place into existence, to make out of ancestors and land an illusion that has the whole world believing we are someone—and somewhere—we are not. This, to her, was as dire a mystery as the predicament of *Ina Kale*.

I think of my great-grandmother when you call me Congolese. It strikes me that you and I are having the same disagreement my ancestors had with yours. You see this place as Congo, and, by consequence, you see me as Congolese. In your eyes I am, in effect, the product of a big jagged line. But there was something here

> before someone set about drawing that line. And that something includes my great-grandmother. Whose memories and whose blood she gave to me. And no amount of ink nor repetition can change that.
>
> So what should you call me instead of Congolese? The great-grandchild of my great-grandmother, keeper of memories, one who stayed, ina kale. Take your pick . . .

But the Belgian did not take his pick. At least, not then. Instead he ordered another round of drinks and stared at the darkening lake.

And that was that.

Except it wasn't. For, though the Nande did not push the point, his story had already perpetrated a rupture, had fingered the rift between his location of residence and his location of belonging, had raised the specter of the transatlantic history that displaced him in his own home. And there they sat, squarely in the rift, the Belgian and the Nande, one in Congo, the other in Yira land, side by side watching the same moon rise over two irreconcilable lands.

THOSE WHO WENT (THAT IS, THOSE WHO WERE TAKEN)

I, too, have great-grandmothers. And mine, too, kept memories.

One of them kept hers in a box. In her box was a letter that traveled across the ocean and into her hands. The letter followed her from Denmark, from whence she came to "America" to reunite with her stowaway husband. Armed with nothing more than a destination, she sold her farm, packed her daughter, and willingly boarded a ship. Her relatives, left behind, sent a letter addressed with the faith of a small town:

> Jennifer Mahler
> San Francisco
> United States of America

And the letter arrived.

In her old age, my grandmother (who was eleven when her mother received this missive) told me of the letter as a story about kindness. She told me about the long list of numbers and streets scrawled then crossed off the worn envelope, the tally of doors before hers tried in vain. As I recall, she told me this, too, as a story about perseverance, about an era in which. In which something. But, try as I might, I cannot remember the end of her thought. Because, no matter how her thought ended (and no matter how much I love her), whatever she said was only true for her. There is, simply, no era in which whatever it was was—or is—also true for me.

For I am also the descendent of those enslaved by fragrant strangers. Of people who never willingly boarded a ship. To whom no one from back home would think to send a letter. Who no one from back home could possibly know existed (who could not be lost because no one was looking for them).[4] Of course they did exist and, through the impenetrable lineage of bondage, eventually begot my (other) great-grandmother. And bequeathed to her the riddle of "freedom."

By the time I intercepted her memories, she was living in Plaquemine, Louisiana, with the bottom half dozen of her daughter's brood (her daughter having marched the eldest west in the second great migration). By then, the rapidly gentrifying neighborhood in which she harbored her grandbabies was predominantly white. They, of course, were entirely Black. A fact her kindly neighbor Mrs. Boudreaux never tired of pointing out. *Here, nigger, come! I've been to market and have extra cabbage for you. Here, nigger, come! Take these shoes, they're used but fit for that growing boy of yours. Here, nigger, come! . . .*

I was always told she meant it kindly, Mrs. Boudreaux. That in her rush to charity it simply never occurred to her to learn my great-grandmother's name. Ironically (and for the record), my great-grandmother's name was Louisa White, hardly a name to defile the virtue of a delicate Southern tongue.

The point, though, is less about names and neighbors than it is about what we discard. And why. Great-Grandma Louisa discarded, for her progeny, the illusion of beneficence, the reflex to sacrifice dignity. Without fail, she collected the goods, thanked Mrs. Boudreaux, and threw them in the trash. Always in front of the children. And that is how they learned to survive the world of Black and white.

So that is what they taught me, my father and a battalion of kin. To listen through the ignorance of pride and stay my course. It just so happens that my course leads back, with the crushing predictability of Sisyphus, to the proverbial Mrs. Boudreaux. To illusions of beneficence, to stories about care, perseverance, and whatever. Stories half my ancestors will unto me and the other half condemn to the trash.

Both are meant as acts of mercy. Both, in their way, lead back to the haunted question of origin—one by virtue of geography, the other by virtue of character. But I cannot help but wonder: What if my great-grandmothers were neighbors? Had they been, I, in all likelihood, would not exist, my viability having been prohibited, for more than four centuries, by "law."

And that, for me, is the rift. It is what leaves me, like the Belgian and the Nande, irreconcilable, suffocating under the "degradation of being divided against myself . . . [under] the polarity of my own vulnerability."[5]

This, then, is my parable: neither the box nor the letter still exists. It is probably not fair to say the letter was discarded, certainly not willfully thrown in the trash. But no one kept it. And that strikes me as an ultimate measure of privilege, of knowing with such inalienable truth that one is both sought and found that one can afford to discard the proof.

In my quest to seek that which is lost, it is significant that only one of my great-grandmothers kept her memories in a box. The other kept hers in blood. And it turns out blood is more reliable than boxes in matters of inheritance. So I inherited the fact of blood and the story of a letter. And I inherited the double vision to know, with trembling cold anger, that, given its unlikely arrival in her hands, Great-Grandma Louisa would have kept such a letter until her dying day. And beyond. Because it would have given her the precious answer to the impenetrable question of where she was from.

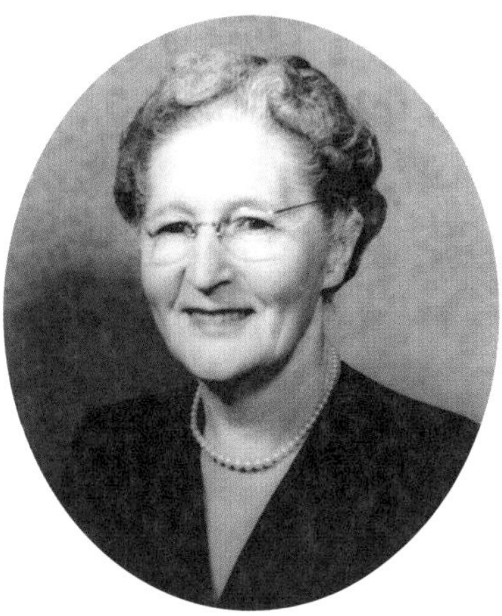

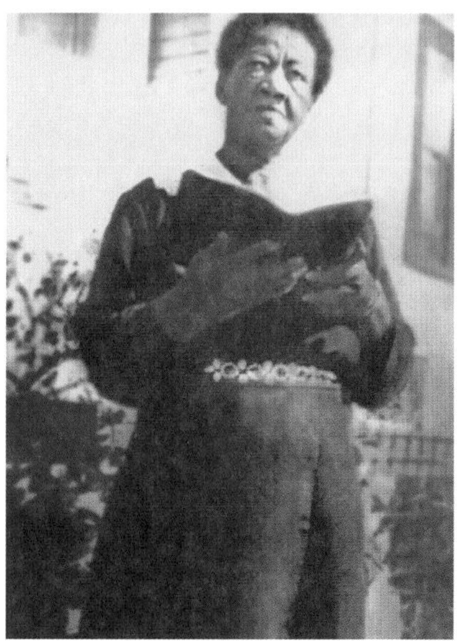

(*above*) Jennifer Marie Mahler

(*right*) Louisa Johnson Harris Wright White

LINES

Two-ness of place, like two-ness of being, is a consequence of lines. As any double-sighted child of diaspora can see, the big jagged line that so tormented the matriarchs of Yira land is close kin to the color line that so tormented their contemporaries an ocean away, that so torments us still. Of course these lines have their differences—one is a function of displacement, the other of disappearance. And though they are both afterbirths of race, they slice differently through geopolitics.

But they have something crucial in common: both lines hold possibility hostage. From children of diaspora they hold ransom the possibility of *inheriting* a "from," for we have been too thoroughly dislocated; from the matriarchs of Yira land they hold ransom the possibility of *bequeathing* a "from," for it has been too thoroughly disappeared.

These possibilities withheld serve as collateral to secure the common demand that we see the world anew. For the displaced, that newness is in blood; for the disappeared, it is in earth. For the children of diaspora, the demand is that, instead of seeing ourselves as daughters and sons of any specific place, we see ourselves as the progeny of pigment. For the Nande and his great-grandmother, the demand is that, instead of seeing Yira land, instead of seeing all the lands, they see—and pledge allegiance to—this thing called Congo.

And make no mistake, this demand is literal. On both sides of the sea. To dispel any inkling of metaphor, to make of race a Truth, searing lines sliced not just through constitutions but through the measure of human blood. And in a parallel choreography of power, to dispel any inkling of metaphor, to make of this thing called Congo a place, the big jagged line sliced not just through a map in Berlin; it sliced clean through Nsala's daughter.

But, unlike displacement that severed us from space, unlike disappearance that confined ancestral lands to the "past," Nsala's daughter's dismemberment was not a possibility withheld but a possibility fulfilled. It was her baptism, however perverse, as citizen of the newly minted nation. That only her limbs and not her body, her head, or her heart were inducted into citizenry is a telling feature of her newfound "from."

I see myself, a child of diaspora, suspended in space and time with the matriarchs of Yira land and with Nsala's daughter. Counterpart to the wall of patriarchs, we form a trilogy of our own, of those for whom the matter of origin has been thrice perverted—by bodies forced through space, by space forced through bodies, by bodies and space asphyxiated in time. And each of us, for our own reasons, is therefore undone by the simple, factual question of where we are from.

In our defense, we are undone because the question of origin is not, in truth, a question of fact but a question of complicity. That is the trap. To answer in terms of place is to answer in terms of lines not of our own making. It is to answer in terms that, for the entirety of transatlantic history, have coerced fiction into fact and vice versa. And, in so doing, have imprisoned us, each in our own way, in the geographies of space, time, and imagination.

Make no mistake, our captivity is neither arbitrary nor accidental. For both lines and facts have antecedents. For the dislocated, the disappeared, and the dismembered, lines and facts have long been malevolent bedfellows proselytizing power through a depraved choreography of "truth."

When God, as a matter of "fact," became white, his interlocutors (in medieval Europe) drew a great—and *divinely* ordained—line dividing celestial from terrestrial, habitable from inhabitable regions. Imagine the chagrin of all for whom divinity was, by definition, not exclusive.

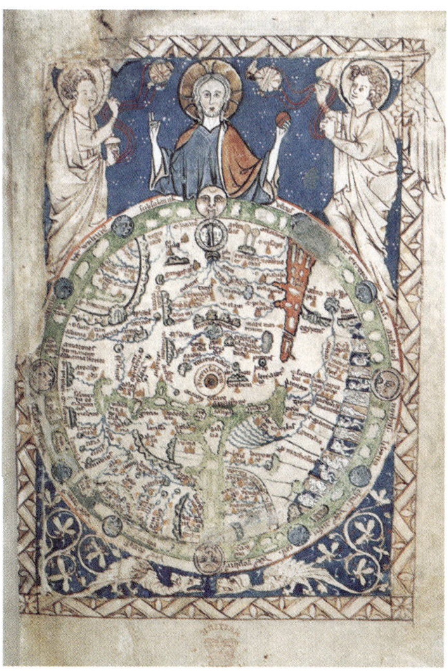

Psalter World Map, ca. 1262

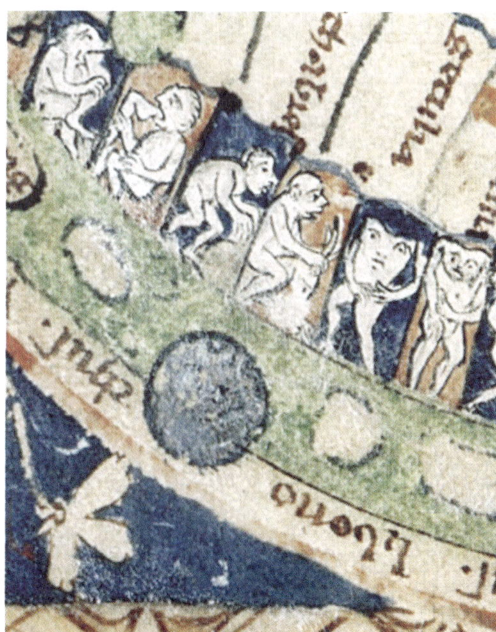

Close-up of the grotesque inhabitants of Central Africa

To enshrine not just the whiteness but, too, the gender of their God, they also drew a great—and *biologically* ordained—line dividing dominance in terms of sex. Imagine the chagrin of all for whom brute force was not a measure of consent.

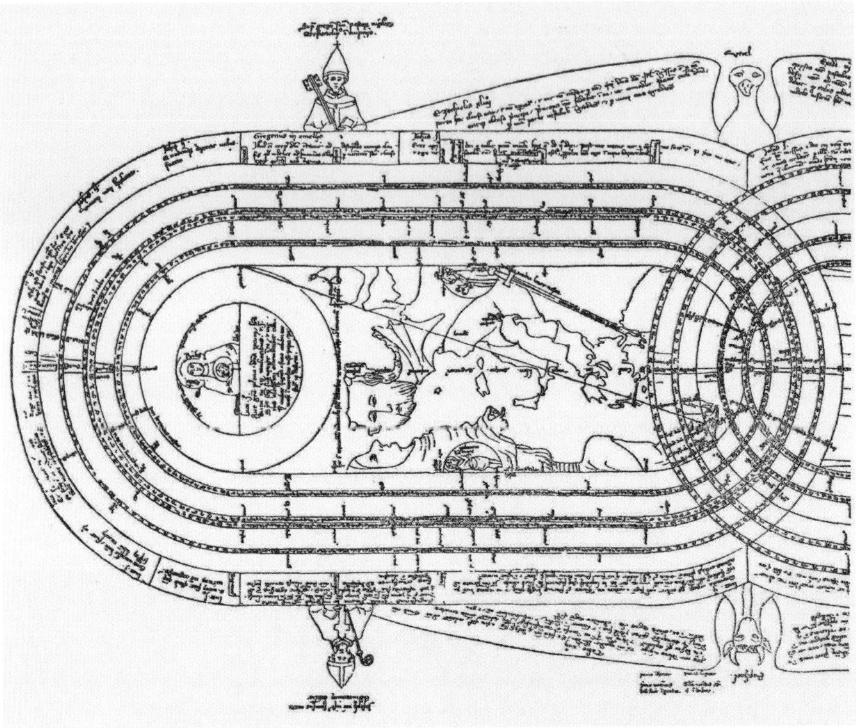

Canistris World Map, 1341, anthropomorphizes Europe as King and Africa as the object of his desire and thus, per gendered norms, his rightful claim.

When, for purposes of commerce, this white, male God became a patron of state, his monarchs (in Renaissance Europe) drew a great—and *commercially* ordained—line dividing the valuable from the invaluable world. Imagine the chagrin of all for whom value was tethered not to currency of coin but to currency of cooperation, community.

(*opposite*) "Amity lines," as designated by the 1559 Treatise of Cateau-Cambrésis between France and Spain, which used the Prime Meridian and the Tropic of Cancer to identify the territory—north and east of the lines—in which the rule of law applied. (Notably, laws applied to people from north and east of the lines regardless of where they were. And vice versa.)

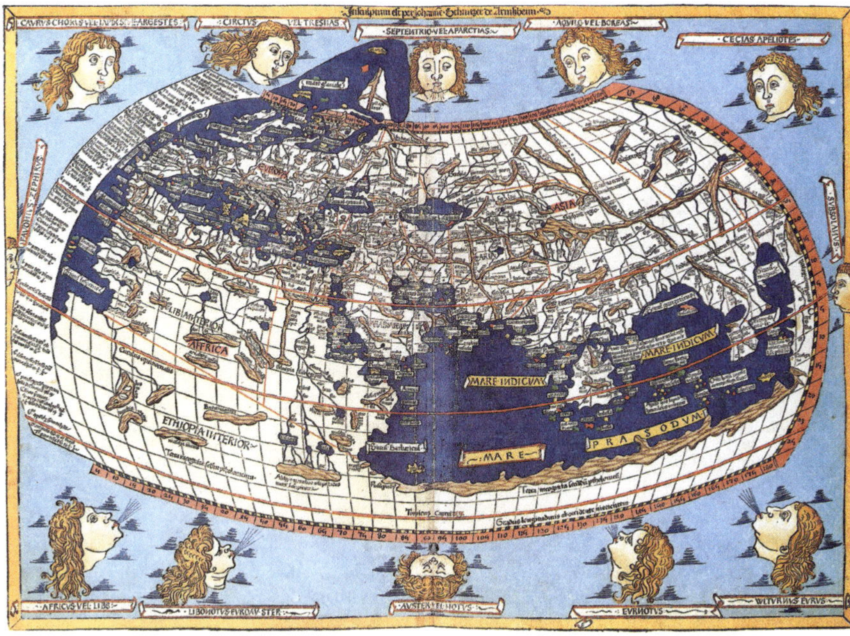

Ptolemy World Map, 1482

When commerce mutated into lust for excess, its patriarchs (in late Renaissance Europe) drew a great—and *legally* ordained—line dividing the "lawful" from the "lawless" lands. Imagine the chagrin of all for whom law was not a slippery mercenary of theft but an honorable barometer of balance.

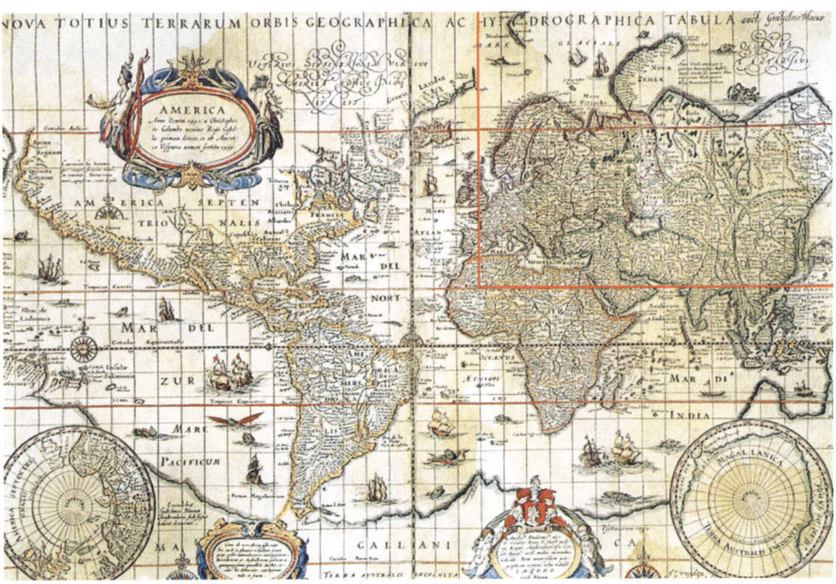

And, when human reason replaced God as the one source of Truth, its intellectuals (in Enlightenment Europe) drew a great—and *scientifically* ordained—line dividing the higher from the lower races. Imagine the chagrin of all for whom knowing was not an act of violence but an act of love.

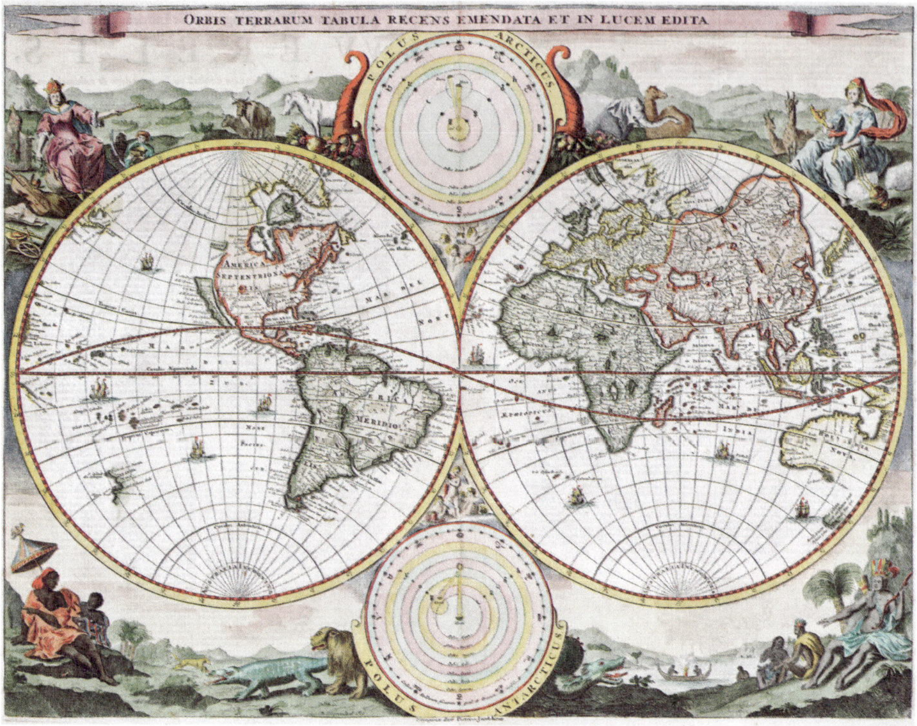

Then, when commerce enlisted science as its evangelist, its mercenaries (in modern Europe and in the "New World") drew all manner of lines dividing all manner of people, places, and things. Imagine the chagrin of all manner of people, places, and things.

(*above*) *Orbis Terrarum Tabula Recens Emendata et in Lucen Edita*, ca. 1663, with hierarchy of races depicted in the corner cartouches (bottom left, of course, being lowest of low).

(*opposite, top*) 1861 map showing the distribution of the slave population (percentage of slaves by county) in the southern United States; produced by the US Coast Survey based on 1860 census data.

(*opposite, bottom*) 1927 map of Lubumbashi (southern Congo), then Elizabethville, with "neutral zone" (*circled*) separating Congolese quarters from European colonial families by a distance greater than either a mosquito or a fly could traverse, thus sparing whites the horrific possibility of being touched by any insect that also touched Black skin. It still exists.

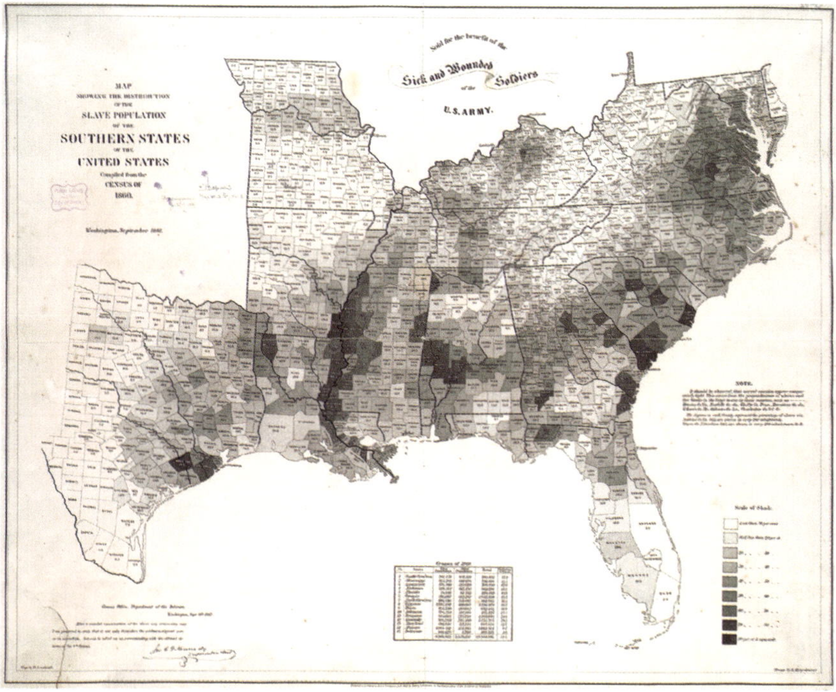
Sold for the benefit of the
Sick and Wounded Soldiers
of the
U.S. ARMY.
MAP
SHOWING THE DISTRIBUTION
OF THE
SLAVE POPULATION
OF THE
SOUTHERN STATES
OF THE
UNITED STATES
Compiled from the
CENSUS OF
1860.
NOTE.
Scale of Shade.

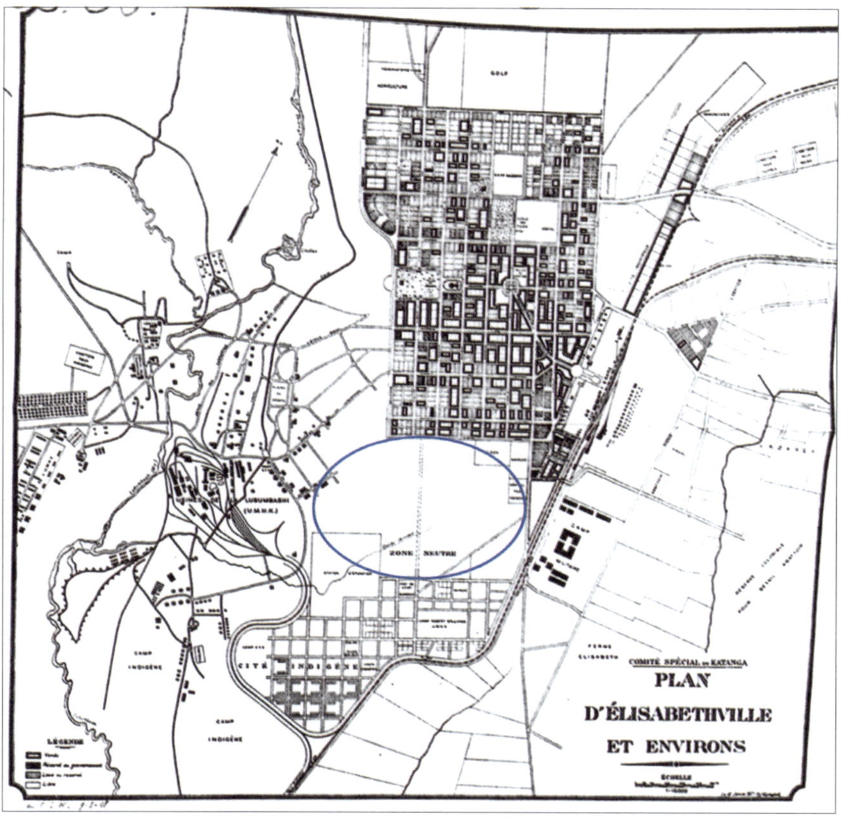
GOLF
LUBUMBASHI
(U.M.H.K.)
ZONE NEUTRE
CITÉ INDIGÈNE
CAMP
INDIGÈNE
CAMP
INDIGÈNE
LÉGENDE
FERME
ELISABETH
COMITÉ SPÉCIAL DU KATANGA
PLAN
D'ÉLISABETHVILLE
ET ENVIRONS
ÉCHELLE

And thus from the deceptive, gluttonous loins of race, patriarchy, and capitalism was born the new world order: lines.

Lines are the genesis of nation. The ironclad illusion that holds possibility hostage, preventing us from inheriting or bequeathing a universe birthed by the mother of creation, Nyamuhanga, as was Yira land. Imprisoned is the memory—and the possibility—of her bounty, of her son, Hangi (providence); her divine spirits Muhima, the healer; Mulimberi, the protector; Nyavandu, mother and guardian of human beings; and Nyavingi, mother of abundance. Imprisoned are the sacred bird, A'kasinimbira; the sacred grain; Ovhùlo, the sacred white sheep; and the values of courage, gratitude, and sacrifice they instill.

To pledge allegiance to this thing called Congo is to pledge allegiance to a different source of existence: *In the beginning was the word and the word was with man. And all things were made through him. In him was greed and his greed was the death of men. And his greed shone in the darkness and the darkness comprehendeth it not.*

It was thus that Congo, like so many places, came to be. Its origin a line penned by a Belgian king in Berlin, slashed through the limbs of Nsala's daughter. Of course, like all lines, the big jagged line of Congo has invisible antecedents that masquerade as fact.

Lines are the genesis of color. The ironclad illusion that holds possibility hostage, preventing us from inheriting or bequeathing a from. Preventing us from knowing where to look, much less what was lost. This is the sleight of hand that imprisons our secrets—and our possibilities—in our veins, yet severs from us the skills of divination to decipher messages in blood. Imprisoned are the stories, the mother tongues, and all the possibilities of being they contain. In their stead are mendacious lines that mutate into borders, nooses, shackles, laws, percentages of blood. In their stead are ghosts.

To pledge allegiance to this thing called race is to pledge allegiance to a different source of existence: *In the beginning was the word and the word was white. And all things were made through the word. In it was the power of invisibility and this power was the death of possibility. And the power created darkness and the darkness . . .*

It was thus that Black, like so many colors, came to be. Its origin a despotic fantasy of power, mutated into lines and slashed through space and time. Of course, like all lines, the mendacious line of color has invisible antecedents that masquerade as fact.

These "facts"—of faith, commerce, law, and science—are the cardinal pillars of the geography of complicity. They are the agents that hold possibility hostage, that negotiate the terms on which we see (or do not see) ourselves in space and time, the ghosts that haunt the question of origin in the aftermath of transatlantic history. They are, thus, the shackles against which we revolt in our simple, factual failure to say, with dignity, where we are from.

To decompose one's way through life is to recognize the many normalized demands to replicate colonial logic. To recognize that they are everywhere. And that none of them is innocent. The very question *Where are you from?* is an insidious demand that we replicate the colonial gaze in the most intimate acts of self-perception. For to answer in terms of place is to endorse the logic of our own dismembering, of our own displacement. It is to brand ourselves with lines and pigment and thus to participate, by force of coercion, in our own undoing. This, in turn, is to refuse, willfully, to look for the possibilities rendered invisible by systems of normalized violence, and, in so doing, to deny the very possibility of seeing Nsala's daughter.

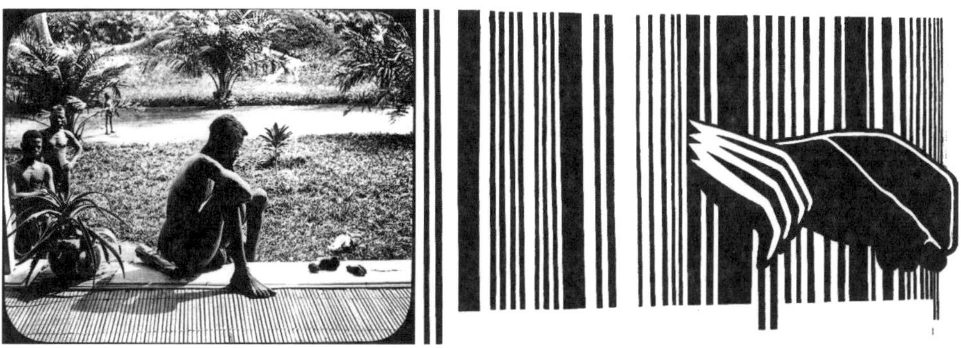

Replicate: Nsala's Daughter

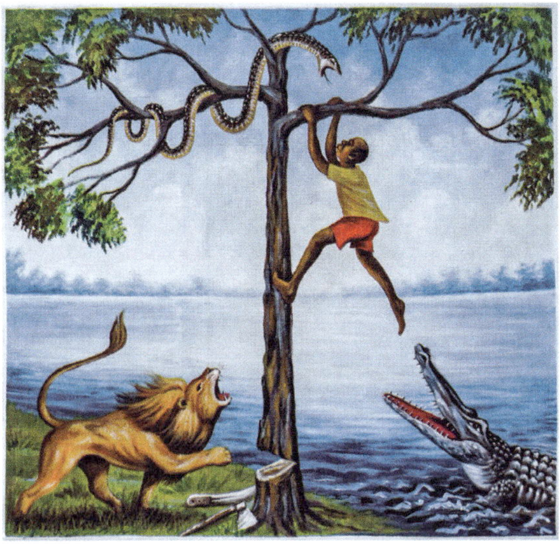

Ina Kale

5. To Contradict

Though I will never know for certain, I suspect the Nande's memory-keeping great-grandmother added ina kale to the trilogy of founding fathers to make a point about invisible possibility. About what the fragrant strangers and their machine-wielding progeny did not see even as they were standing in the midst of it. They could not, for instance, see the possibility of Yira land, or any land, existing outside the past. So, in the name of progress, they anointed themselves gods and created The State.

Their legacy is plain to see. Congo, replete with constitution and insignia of state, is corroborated on all the world's maps. It is a place to be, to be from. And, since its genesis in Berlin, Congo has accrued a tumultuous succession of upheavals that pass for history: five name changes, countless political assassinations, endless wars, thefts, precarities, violences, all carried out, faithfully, in the name of progress. Along the way, there have been visionary and heroic figures—matriarchs and patriarchs alike; there have been popular masses willing to risk ultimate sacrifice contesting the symptoms of the big jagged line. But their dreams, like their Black bodies, have been crushed between the predictable cogs of Christianity and commerce.

The same is true on the other side of the sea, where Black bodies and dreams, menaced by consanguine lines, are crushed between the predictable cogs of color and capital. Indeed, any double-sighted child of diaspora can see that ina kale is not a parable of Congo per se, but rather a story about every corner of Nyamuhanga's green earth enslaved to lines that slice clear through its daughters and their fathers, its mothers and their sons.

I could name many. The point, though, is not a list but the practice of decomposing; the point is what we see when we look for possibilities rendered invisible by systems of normalized violence. Of course, to see invisible possibilities we must, first, see the systems that obscure them. We must see them not as Reality—not, that is, as laws (those unbreakable truths of nature); we must see them actively and explicitly as rules, as calculated choices of human beings.

This is a matter of recognizing the geography of complicity, the "facts"—of faith, commerce, law, and science—that hold possibility hostage. It is, too, a matter of seeing that holding possibility hostage not only dictates the terms of space and time, but also of imagination. Indeed, in this big breaking world, the geography of complicity is aided and abetted by the geography of imagination, by the assumption that seeing is believing, that the unnameable does not or cannot exist.

To contradict, in the practice of decomposing the colonial gaze, is to confront the many forces that condition our perception. To confront them with sights set on unmasking systems that substitute for Reality. It is to meditate, deeply, on ina kale; to recognize, in all its forms, the reflex to seek refuge from the lion in the jaws of the crocodile, to shackle imagination to a half-hewn tree. And this begins with a ruthless analysis of history not as Truth, but as the pernicious coagulation of collective illusions.

ACCOMPLICES

It is no secret that Nsala's daughter happens to be my particular ghost. Her haunting has taught me to see that two-ness of place, like two-ness of being, is a consequence of lines. No one knows this better than she, whose two-ness—of both place *and* being—is literal, her limbs inducted into Congo, the rest of her discarded in her ancestral land. Even to me, a daughter of diaspora born of strange Southern fruit, her two-ness adds a cold trembling to the familiar sensation of dislocation.

But there is more to her story. Her two-ness is a consequence of lines that imprisoned her in geographies of space and time. But equally lethal is her incarceration in the geography of imagination. And for that she required an accomplice. To become, by virtue of her dismemberment, a symbol of nation, she had not only to be mutilated but also to be documented; she—or what little of her was conscripted to state—had to be transposed into an image that could circumnavigate the globe and, in its wake, congeal in the collective imaginary the fact of a place called Congo.[1]

Of course her image was not the only evangelist of nation. Like lines and facts, images have antecedents. And while their status may be privileged for their capacity of deception, they are but one in a genealogy of technologies that coerce fiction into "truth" in the world of lines.[2] In the case of Nsala's daughter, her image was preceded by treaties and decrees that "formally" bled the land from her ancestors, flags and institutions that christened it anew, the accoutrements of "law" and "justice" to surveil—and acquit—the parade of "progress."

Each in its own way, these agents of complicity unleashed a lethal elixir of righteousness and "truth." In their quest to make of Yira land, of all the lands, this thing called Congo, the zealots armed themselves with the gilded words of faith, commerce, law, and science:

By encouraging the native propensity for trade, the advantages that might be derived in a commercial point of view are incalculable; nor should we lose sight of the inestimable blessings it is in our power to bestow upon the unenlightened African, by giving him the light of Christianity. Those two pioneers of civilization—Christianity and commerce—should ever be inseparable, said Scottish missionary David Livingstone.[3]

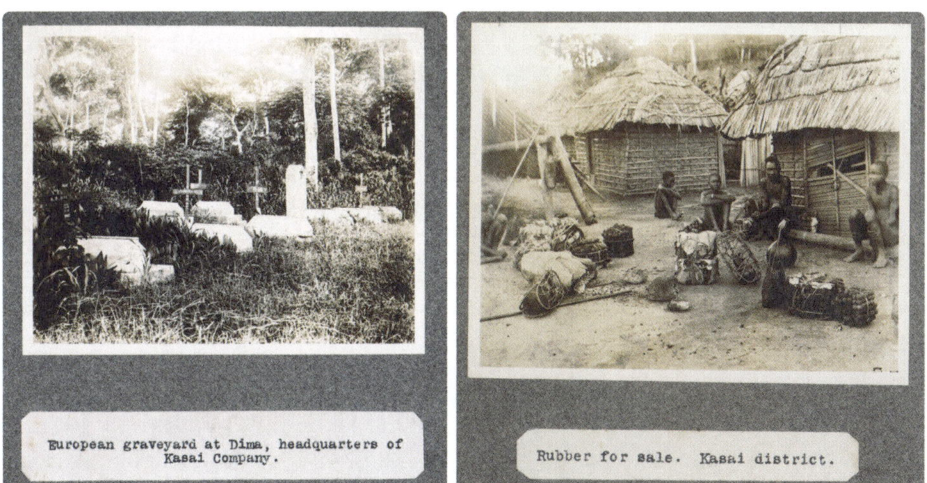

death, forced conversion, capitalist extraction

"Inestimable Blessings"

The discoveries due to the daring explorers permit us to say from this day that it [Central Africa] is one of the most beautiful and the richest countries created by God. The Conference of Brussels has nominated an Executive Committee to carry into execution [the] declaration and resolutions . . . of an International Association to . . . tear aside the veil of darkness which still enshrouds Central Africa. . . . We boldly affirm that all those who desire the enfranchisement of the black races are interested in our success, said Belgian king Léopold II.[4]

Aye! said Europe.[5]

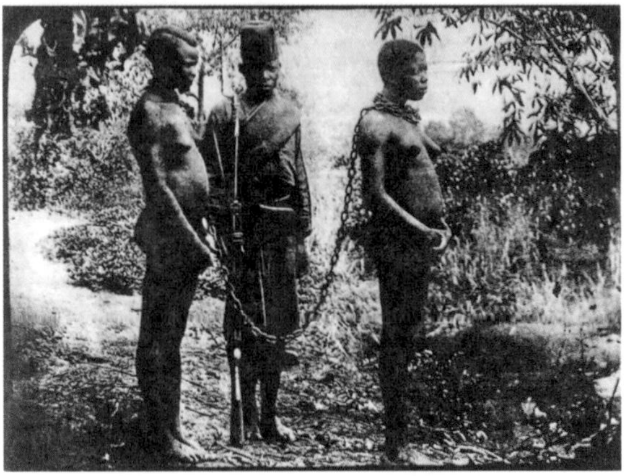

"Enfranchisement of Black Races"

women taken hostage after their husbands

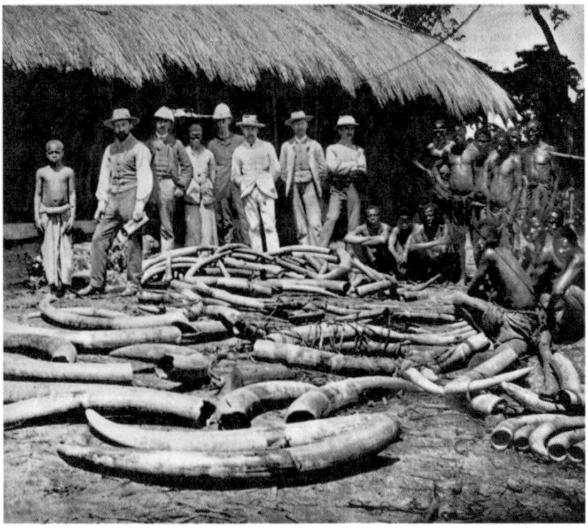

"Tearing aside the Veil of Darkness"

a small portion of the ~2,500 tons of ivory Leopold

And, thus impassioned, the experts, the philanthropes, and the pious anointed themselves angels of redemption and set out to remake the heart of Africa in their own image. In league with the depraved choreography of Truth, they coerced facts of wealth and power into fictions of abolitionism, enfranchisement, and blessing. And, in the name of God (and commerce!), they clawed at the veil of darkness enshrouding Nsala's daughter.

More precisely, they clawed right through Nsala's daughter. The veil is another matter entirely. The veil, a familiar conceit, is the progenitor of second sight among outcasts rendered strangers in our own homes.[6] It is a defining line in a blueprint of deception that makes of one place two. With its curious math—one drop, limbs divided by torso, double vision for three-fifths a man—it made of Yira land, like "freedom" land, a house of slaves.

A house of slaves. That is the common denominator. Perhaps not a perfect metaphor for nation, but far from an imperfect one, for it makes seeable the otherwise chimerical architecture of state. This place called Congo, begot of commerce and of church, has all the trappings of the citadels of slavery. It rests squarely on the foundation of capital; it has, as walls, boundaries policed by violence; the struggle of writhing Black bodies is exorcised from view in the elevated quarters of the elite, whose churches and marketplaces sanctify their founding doctrine, consecrating and reconsecrating the union of Christianity and commerce in the name of civilization:

To the Secretary of State of the Congo Free State,

The Free State was created, with the consent of the entire world, twenty years ago, by a single will . . . in the object of opening central Africa to civilisation. . . . Its origin came from the acquiescence of the native chiefs and the personal efforts of its creator. (In the beginning was the word and the word was with man . . .)

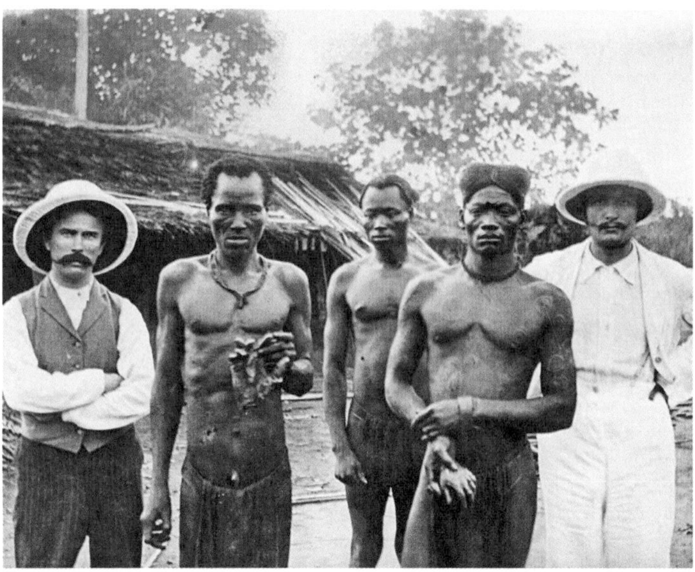

British missionaries with Congolese holding severed hands of two men murdered by sentinels of the Anglo-Belgian Indian Rubber Company

"Acquiescence"

In these regions which twenty years ago were still plunged in the most frightful barbarism and which had been crossed by only a few whites at the cost of superhuman efforts, met at every moment by the arrows of hostile people; in these districts where the tribes . . . fought each other without cessation and without mercy . . . —in this dark and mysterious continent the State has been constituted and organized with marvelous rapidity, introducing into the heart of Africa the benefits of civilisation. (And all things were made through him . . .)

> *The villages, which call to mind our attractive sea-side towns, are numerous along the banks of the great river, and the two terminals of the Lower Congo Railway . . . remind one of the industrial cities of Europe. The railway . . . carried to the heart of the equatorial belt, the 24 steamers which float upon the Congo and its tributaries, the regular service of the postal communication, the telegraph lines that amount to 1200 kilometers, the hospitals established in the principle places, all of these things born of yesterday, give travelers the impression that they are in a country which has long enjoyed the blessings of European civilisation, and not in one which but a quarter of a century ago was totally unknown and savage. It makes one wonder what magic power or firm will, aided by heroic efforts, was able to so change a country in such a short time.*[7]

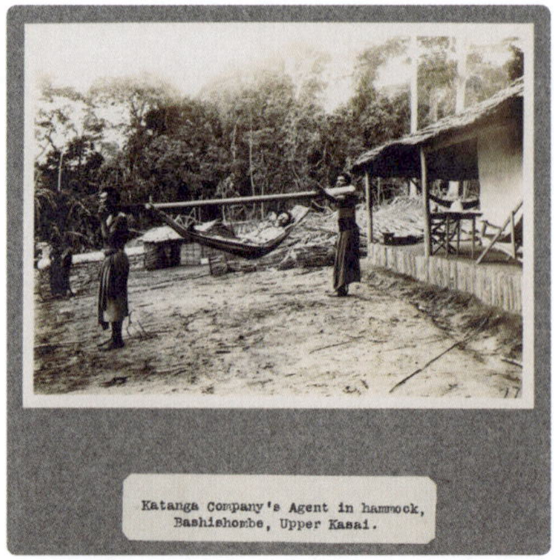

"Superhuman Efforts of Whites"

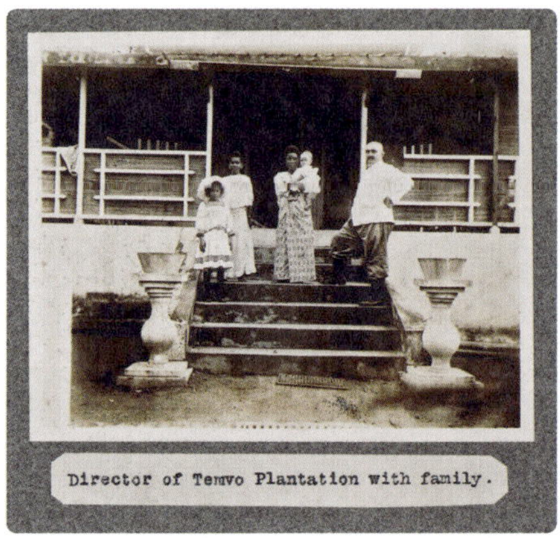

"Magic Power, Firm Will"

Here, in plain sight, the blueprint of a house of slaves, the genealogy of technologies that civilized the life right out of ten million million broken Black bodies. These are the machines—of transport and transmission—that coerce fiction into truth.

In the case of Congo there were, of course, quibbles about degrees of fiction and truth. But that is but a footnote in the story of Nsala's daughter. What matters is that—and how—she was imprisoned in the geography of imagination.

Dissent was a first-degree accomplice. It unleashed a wave of moral outrage. Pamphlets decried the plight of the "native who has been deprived by Royal Decree of his rights as a land-owner . . . and has become *de facto* a serf."[8] Reports condemned the "cruelty and oppression" and "forced taxation" imposed on natives–turned–slaves of empire.[9] Studies noted that "with the abolition of the legal form of slavery the economic substance has not disappeared."[10] And, riding the tides of civilizing machines, these and other outcries unleashed a wave of righteous dissent.

And then came the camera.

It is, in certain circles, a source of pride that the camera made its way to Congo in the hands of a woman. It is, in other circles, a source of inspiration that the photographs taken by that woman advanced an international call for "justice."

I am not of those circles. I laud matriarchal lineages and the impulse to enact change, but that is not what I see in these photographs. Make no mistake, I understand that the intentions of their author were noble, that her sense of morality compelled her to expose the collateral damage wrought by a despot. But to this daughter of diaspora, these photographs evoke, to complete our architecture of enslavement, that symbol of finality and rupture: the door of no return. They are a last glimpse of a beloved home foreclosed of possibility by the firm-willed constitution of The State.

Worse, these photographs are complicit in the extinction of possibility. For all their zeal to procure "justice" in the heart of Africa, they dispossess us—on both sides of the veil—of the possibility of seeing, much less inhabiting, any place other than The State. By the campaigns they buoyed through Europe and the United States, they congealed in the global imagination, the one and only way of seeing this place: Congo. Even as their civilizing energies seized, full force, on Léopold's barbarity, they could not conceive of any greater good than to transfer deed of "ownership" of this vast land from the hands of an almighty man to the hands of an almighty state. So allegiant were they to the world begot of faith, commerce, law, and science that any other conception of space was, like the torso of Nsala's daughter, quite literally, outside their frame of vision.

MY FATHER'S WOMB

I, too, am imprisoned in the geography of imagination, my ability to see (or not to see) myself in space and time conditioned by peculiar fictions coerced into Truth. The accomplices, in my case, are an accumulation of extraordinary measures taken to prevent my being. Not mine alone (nor mine per se) but any threat to the absolute omnipotence—and purity—of "race."

Save for the cold trembling, it would seem a farce: the great energies unleashed to legislate sperm, to extinguish the possibility of "a mongrel breed of citizens."[11] But it was, and remains, a deathly serious business.

In my quest to see the dead, this leads back, with crushing predictability, to the haunted question of origin, *What if my great-grandmothers had been neighbors?* The answer, like all collective illusions, has antecedents:

In 1664, the marriage of my father to my mother would have condemned her to a life of slavery (his status a foregone conclusion):

Be it further enacted by the authority advice and consent aforesaid that whatsoever freeborn woman shall intermarry with any slave . . . shall serve the master of such slave during the life of her husband, and that the [children] of such freeborn women so married shall be slaves as their fathers were.[12]

The same sin in reverse (that is, had he instead of she worn white skin) would have been an economic boon, the progeny of Black rape being chattel:

Whereas some doubts have arisen whether children got by any Englishman upon a negro woman shall be slave or free, Be it therefore enacted . . . that all children borne in this country shall be held bond or free only according to the condition of the mother.[13]

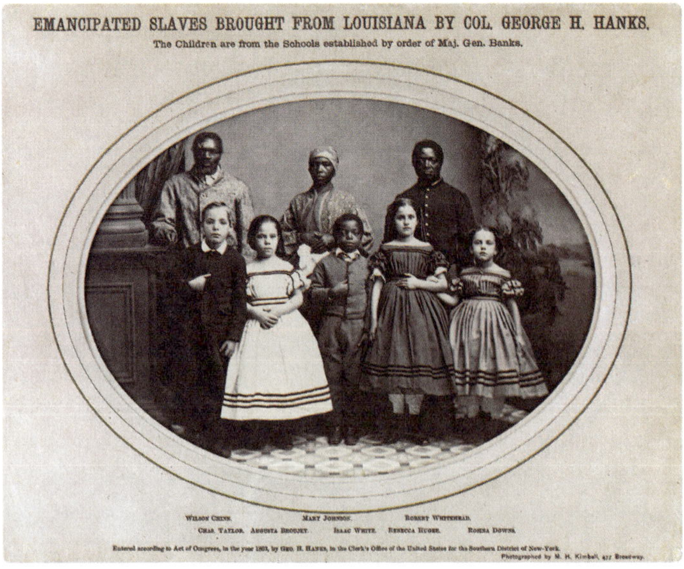

By 1691 their marriage would have been prohibited entirely, regardless of who wore which skin:

For prevention of that abominable mixture and spurious [children] which hereafter may increase in this dominion, as well as by negroes, mulattos, and Indians intermarrying with English, or other white women, as by their unlawful accompanying with one another,

Be it enacted . . . that . . . whatsoever English or other white man or woman being free, shall intermarry with a negro, mulatto, or Indian man or woman bond or free shall within three months after such marriage be banished and removed from this dominion forever.[14]

But greed (and lust) overpower rules. And thus after centuries of blood shed for patriarchy, a quick about-face to assure that the progeny of Black rape remains chattel:

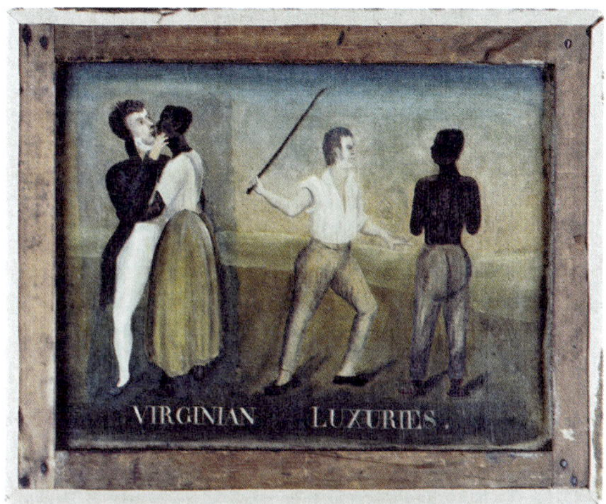

Partus sequitur ventrem (that which is brought forth follows the womb) . . .

And rules (and faith) are lucrative:

And be it further enacted . . . that if any English woman being free shall have a bastard child by any negro or mulatto, she pay the sum of fifteen pounds sterling, within one month after such bastard child shall be born, to the Church wardens of the parish . . . and in default of such payment she shall be taken into the possession of the said Church wardens and disposed of for five years, and the said fine of fifteen pounds, or whatever the woman shall be disposed of for, shall be paid, one third part to their majesties . . . and one other third part to the use of the parish . . . and the other third part to the informer, and that such bastard child be bound out as a servant by the said Church wardens until he or she shall attain the age of thirty yeares, and in case such English woman that shall have such bastard child be a servant, she shall be sold by the said church wardens (after her time is expired that she ought by law serve her master), for five years, and the money she shall be sold for divided as if before appointed, and the child to serve as aforesaid.[15]

With time arose, for some, a nagging question of morality regarding ownership of human beings. And, having held such laws some centuries, there were those who sought repeal, which, in turn, spawned titillating nouns:

Hypodescent; miscegenation . . . !

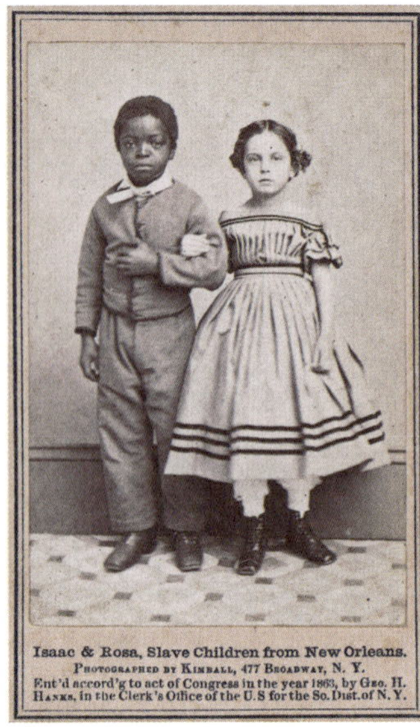

Two New Orleans slave children, c. 1863

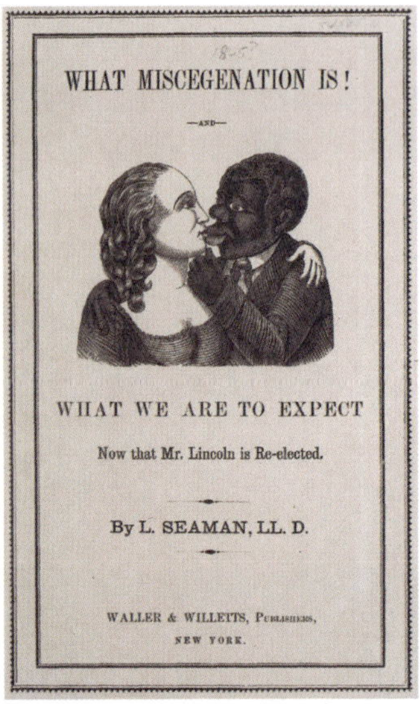
WHAT MISCEGENATION IS!

—AND—

WHAT WE ARE TO EXPECT

Now that Mr. Lincoln is Re-elected.

By L. SEAMAN, LL. D.

WALLER & WILLETTS, Publishers,
NEW YORK.

Then came constitutional amendments:

1865: *Neither slavery nor involuntary servitude, except as a punishment for crime whereof the party shall have been duly convicted, shall exist within the United States, or any place subject to their jurisdiction.*[16]

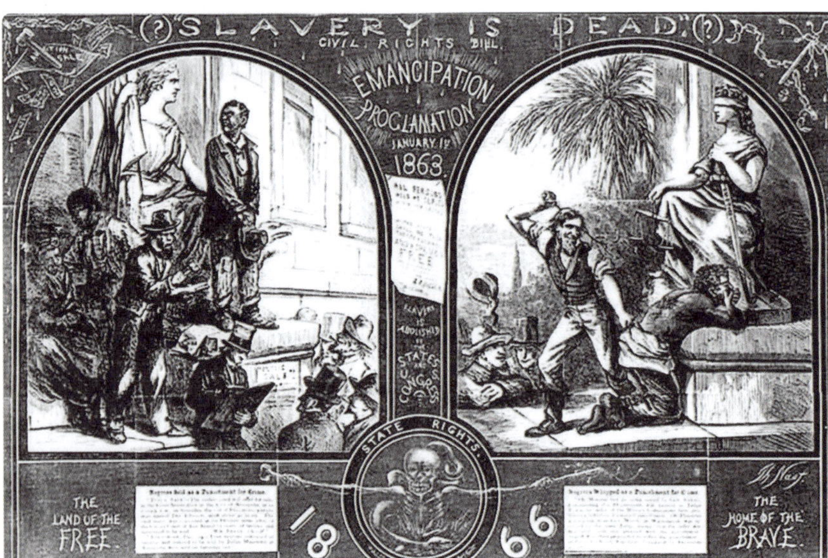

(?) *Slaver Is Dead* (

(see note 16 to this chapter)

1868: *No state shall make or enforce any law which shall abridge the privileges or immunities of citizens of the United States; nor shall any state deprive any person of life, liberty, or property, without due process of law; nor deny to any person within its jurisdiction the equal protection of the laws.*[17]

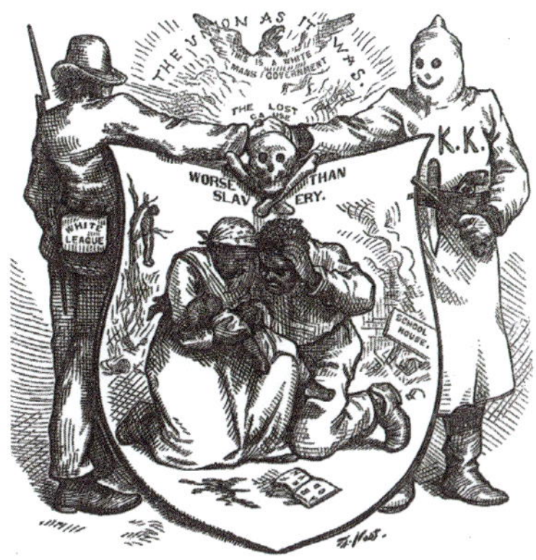

The Union as It Was, the Lost Cause, Worse than Slavery

But in 1883, my parents' marriage could still, in the eyes of the law, merit incarceration:

If any white person and any negro, or the descendant of any negro to the third generation, inclusive, though one ancestor of each generation was a white person, intermarry or live in adultery or fornication with each other, each of them must, on conviction, be imprisoned in the penitentiary or sentenced to hard labor for the county for not less than two nor more than seven years.[18]

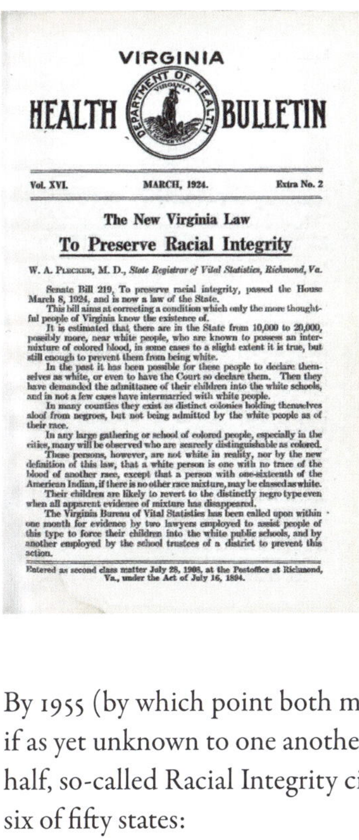

VIRGINIA HEALTH BULLETIN

Vol. XVI. MARCH, 1924. Extra No. 2

The New Virginia Law

To Preserve Racial Integrity

W. A. PLECKER, M. D., *State Registrar of Vital Statistics, Richmond, Va.*

Senate Bill 219, To preserve racial integrity, passed the House March 8, 1924, and is now a law of the State.

This bill aims at correcting a condition which only the more thoughtful people of Virginia know the existence of.

It is estimated that there are in the State from 10,000 to 20,000, possibly more, near white people, who are known to possess an intermixture of colored blood, in some cases to a slight extent it is true, but still enough to prevent them from being white.

In the past it has been possible for these people to declare themselves as white, or even to have the Court so declare them. Then they have demanded the admittance of their children into the white schools, and in not a few cases have intermarried with white people.

In many counties they exist as distinct colonies holding themselves aloof from negroes, but not being admitted by the white people as of their race.

In any large gathering or school of colored people, especially in the cities, many will be observed who are scarcely distinguishable as colored.

These persons, however, are not white in reality, nor by the new definition of this law, that a white person is one with no trace of the blood of another race, except that a person with one-sixteenth of the American Indian, if there is no other race mixture, may be classed as white.

Their children are likely to revert to the distinctly negro type even when all apparent evidence of mixture has disappeared.

The Virginia Bureau of Vital Statistics has been called upon within one month for evidence by two lawyers employed to assist people of this type to force their children into the white public schools, and by another employed by the school trustees of a district to prevent this action.

Entered as second class matter July 28, 1908, at the Postoffice at Richmond, Va., under the Act of July 16, 1894.

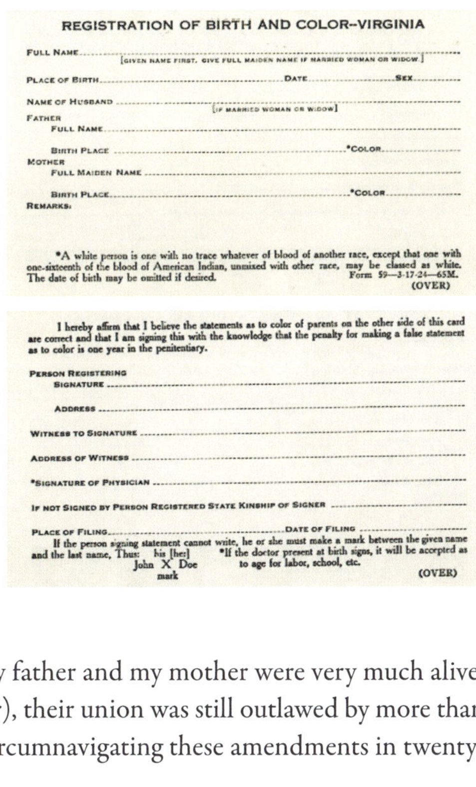

REGISTRATION OF BIRTH AND COLOR--VIRGINIA

FULL NAME ....
[GIVEN NAME FIRST. GIVE FULL MAIDEN NAME IF MARRIED WOMAN OR WIDOW.]

PLACE OF BIRTH .... DATE .... SEX ....

NAME OF HUSBAND ....
[IF MARRIED WOMAN OR WIDOW]

FATHER
FULL NAME ....
BIRTH PLACE .... *COLOR ....

MOTHER
FULL MAIDEN NAME ....
BIRTH PLACE .... *COLOR ....

REMARKS:

*A white person is one with no trace whatever of blood of another race, except that one with one-sixteenth of the blood of American Indian, unmixed with other race, may be classed as white. The date of birth may be omitted if desired. Form 59—3-17-24—65M.

(OVER)

I hereby affirm that I believe the statements as to color of parents on the other side of this card are correct and that I am signing this with the knowledge that the penalty for making a false statement as to color is one year in the penitentiary.

PERSON REGISTERING
SIGNATURE ....
ADDRESS ....

WITNESS TO SIGNATURE ....

ADDRESS OF WITNESS ....

*SIGNATURE OF PHYSICIAN ....

IF NOT SIGNED BY PERSON REGISTERED STATE KINSHIP OF SIGNER ....

PLACE OF FILING .... DATE OF FILING ....

If the person signing statement cannot write, he or she must make a mark between the given name and the last name, Thus: his [her] John X Doe mark

*If the doctor present at birth signs, it will be accepted as to age for labor, school, etc.

(OVER)

By 1955 (by which point both my father and my mother were very much alive, if as yet unknown to one another), their union was still outlawed by more than half, so-called Racial Integrity circumnavigating these amendments in twenty-six of fifty states:

Any negro man and white woman, or any white man and negro woman, who are not married to each other, who shall habitually live in and occupy in the night-time the same room shall each be punished by imprisonment not exceeding twelve months, or by fine not exceeding five hundred dollars.[19]

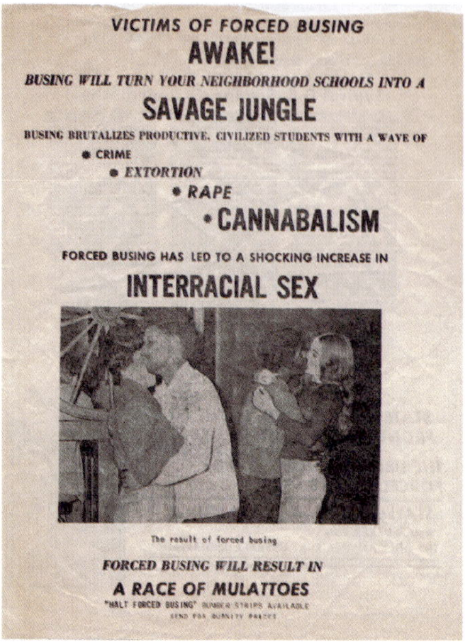

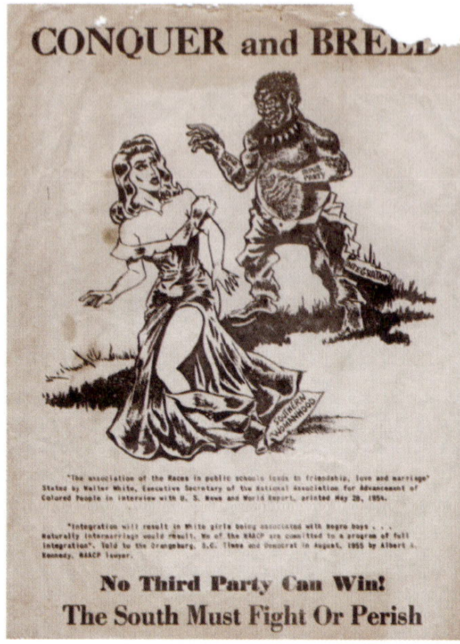

And, by 1959, according to the law, God was still to blame:

Almighty God created the races white, black, yellow, malay and red, and he placed them on separate continents. And, but for the interference with his arrangement, there would be no cause for such marriage. The fact that he separated the races shows that he did not intend for the races to mix.[20]

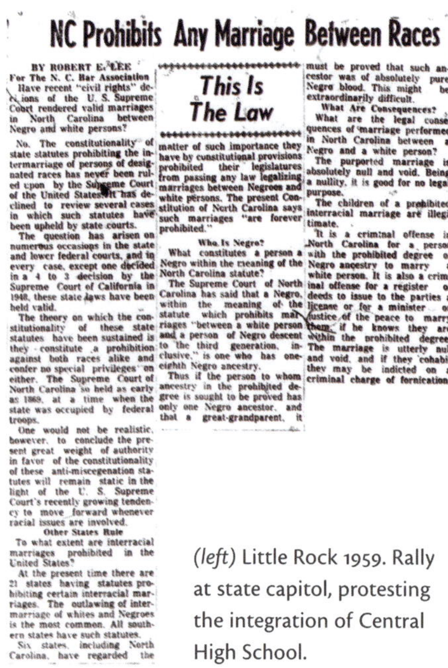

NC Prohibits Any Marriage Between Races

BY ROBERT E. LEE
For The N. C. Bar Association

Have recent "civil rights" decisions of the U. S. Supreme Court rendered valid marriages in North Carolina between Negro and white persons?

No. The constitutionality of state statutes prohibiting the intermarriage of persons of designated races has never been ruled upon by the Supreme Court of the United States. It has declined to review several cases in which such statutes have been upheld by state courts.

The question has arisen on numerous occasions in the state and lower federal courts, and in every case, except one decided in a 4 to 3 decision by the Supreme Court of California in 1948, these state laws have been held valid.

The theory on which the constitutionality of these state statutes have been sustained is they constitute a prohibition against both races alike and confer no special privileges on either. The Supreme Court of North Carolina so held as early as 1869, at a time when the state was occupied by federal troops.

One would not be realistic, however, to conclude the present great weight of authority in favor of the constitutionality of these anti-miscegenation statutes will remain static in the light of the U. S. Supreme Court's recently growing tendency to move forward whenever racial issues are involved.

Other States Rule

To what extent are interracial marriages prohibited in the United States?

At the present time there are 21 states having statutes prohibiting certain interracial marriages. The outlawing of intermarriage of whites and Negroes is the most common. All southern states have such statutes.

Six states, including North Carolina, have regarded the

This Is The Law

matter of such importance they have by constitutional provisions prohibited their legislatures from passing any law legalizing marriages between Negroes and white persons. The present Constitution of North Carolina says such marriages "are forever prohibited."

Who Is Negro?

What constitutes a person a Negro within the meaning of the North Carolina statute?

The Supreme Court of North Carolina has said that a Negro, within the meaning of the statute which prohibits marriages "between a white person and a person of Negro descent to the third generation, inclusive," is one who has one-eighth Negro ancestry.

Thus if the person to whom ancestry in the prohibited degree is sought to be proved has only one Negro ancestor, and that a great-grandparent, it must be proved that such ancestor was of absolutely pure Negro blood. This might be extraordinarily difficult.

What Are Consequences?

What are the legal consequences of marriage performed in North Carolina between a Negro and a white person?

The purported marriage is absolutely null and void. Being a nullity, it is good for no legal purpose.

The children of a prohibited interracial marriage are illegitimate.

It is a criminal offense in North Carolina for a person with the prohibited degree of Negro ancestry to marry a white person. It is also a criminal offense for a register of deeds to issue to the parties a license or for a minister or justice of the peace to marry them, if he knows they are within the prohibited degree. The marriage is utterly null and void, and if they cohabit they may be indicted on a criminal charge of fornication.

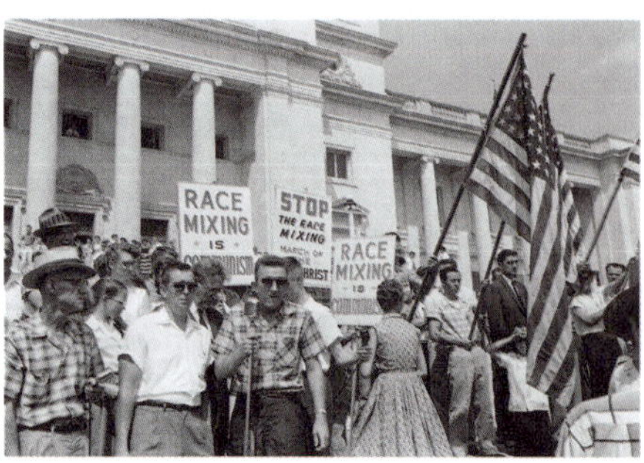

(left) Little Rock 1959. Rally at state capitol, protesting the integration of Central High School.

Setting aside, for now, the question of who interfered with "God's arrangement," and in what interest, let me conclude with this: By 1973, when they happened to marry, my parents' union was, in theory, a national fact (courtesy of the Lovings, the Supreme Court, and the post-Brown politics of 1967).[21] But it took until 2008, another one-and-forty years, to purge miscegenation law from all the books.[22] And even after, clerks refuse—for disclosing race remains a prerequisite of marriage.[23] Not everywhere, but still.

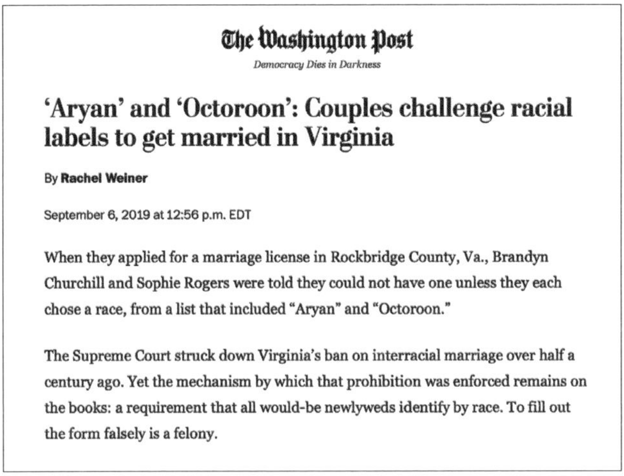

The Washington Post

Democracy Dies in Darkness

'Aryan' and 'Octoroon': Couples challenge racial labels to get married in Virginia

By **Rachel Weiner**

September 6, 2019 at 12:56 p.m. EDT

When they applied for a marriage license in Rockbridge County, Va., Brandyn Churchill and Sophie Rogers were told they could not have one unless they each chose a race, from a list that included "Aryan" and "Octoroon."

The Supreme Court struck down Virginia's ban on interracial marriage over half a century ago. Yet the mechanism by which that prohibition was enforced remains on the books: a requirement that all would-be newlyweds identify by race. To fill out the form falsely is a felony.

These are the rules—and the stakes—that legislate perception. As they evolved they fueled the pesky task of policing blood (just how much Black does it take? a quarter? an eighth? a sixteenth? a sixty-fourth? a drop.). I confess I have, at times, taken solace in the math, in the unwavering certainty of half. But still these facts make of me a curious problem.[24] In the eyes of the law, they make me undeniably, unquestionably, and obviously Black. In the eyes of my beholders, however, my Blackness is another conceit. To some it is self-evident, but to others it is invisible, not all perceptions being legislated by the "remarkable legal point of view which obtains in the United States."[25]

I plead my own case here because the extraordinary measures taken to prevent a "mongrel breed" expose the architecture of the geography of imagination in a land begot of race. Our very existence underscores the impossibility—and absurdity—of conflating laws with rules. The laws (of nature) are crystal clear on the matter of human reproduction. And they have nothing to do with race or color. The rules, by contrast, coerce these peculiar fictions (of race and color) into facts not by virtue of any innate truth but by virtue of repetition. And violence. Indeed, to be Black is not only a depraved equation of blood but also an accumulated experience, inherited and bequeathed.

And that is the trap. The experience is real, in all its intimate ferocity—from chattel to pride—the experience of race is excruciatingly, blessedly real. But in the absence of vigilance (and ghosts), its very realness corroborates the congealing of foundational fictions into an illusion of Reality—that is, the one *and only* possibility of being. Thus rule calcifies into law and we become prisoners to the geography of a very specific imagination.

I find myself mired in this trap with crushing predictability. For as my light-skinned, long-locked body moves through time and space I collide, regularly, with the cold trembling edges of this imagination. Outside the bounds of lines legislated by hypodescent, I find myself clinging to the very definitions I abhor, asserting, for dear life, the fact of mongrel Blackness to ward off ambiguity in the eyes of those whose perceptions are not attuned to race. I assert (or demand, or implore, as the case may be) not because of any delusion that I can overwrite history's death grip on perception, but rather because arming myself with the reality of race is the only means I have to defend my inheritance, to be my father's daughter.

TOXIC SOLIDARITY

One does not need to see Nsala's daughter to see that something is wrong. Seeing her father is enough for that. Seeing a man repaid for slave labor with the severed limbs of his child signals, in the eyes of many, that something is amiss. And, to the more intrepid, it is a call to action.

To Alice Seeley Harris and her accomplices in King Léopold's Congo, Nsala's plight was a rallying cry, fodder for the abolition of one particular dictatorship, for the transfer of life and property to the hallowed hands of The State. Hers is a familiar reflex, an urge to redress injustice, to flex rage and ride the indignant tide of change. This same reflex, a sea away, proclaimed emancipation, abolished one particular institution and shuffled life and property to the hands of a different State. Both were done in the name of moral victory—the righteous outrage that turned the tides of Congo's fate, its antecedent abolitionism that boiled into monumentally uncivil war. And both, in the name of moral victory, are deified by history.

But in the practice of decomposing the colonial gaze, these reflexes—and the campaigns they buoy through time and space—are proof and consequence of the lethal impotence of contradiction. For all her righteous outrage, Ms. Harris, like her abolitionist compatriots, never questioned the ordination of racial hierarchy (much less the whiteness of the God who placed them on top). Nor did the patriarchs of race, including the proclaimer of emancipation, doubt the ordination of white supremacy (much less the inevitability of white rule).[26]

These ills, invisible, were not the target of their ire. (Better said, they could not be "ills" because, in the geography of complicity, they are simply "facts.") Instead they fixed their sights on visible violence—the public chopping, and breaking, and hanging of Black bodies, for instance—hell bent on reforming lamentable glitches in what was, in their eyes, an otherwise laudable system. Ina kale, from lion to crocodile.

This is toxic solidarity: the deployment of dissent in the name of a morality blinded by allegiance to systems of normalized violence. It is the lethal marriage of righteous outrage over symptoms with willful refusal to recognize cause.

To decompose one's way through life is to recognize that, like the demand to replicate, the reflex to contradict takes many forms. Including toxic solidarity. Blinded by allegiance to systems of normalized violence, in the aftermath of transatlantic history contradiction is lasciviously unleashed to abolish symptoms yet rarely trained on the foundational matter of cause. Take Nsala, for instance, whose symptoms (the mutilation and murder of family) were redressed with the privilege of colonial domination (under which mutilation and murder claim a more civilized guise). Or take my own light-skinned, long-locked dilemma: my right to exist, on paper, is a debt of gratitude to one who sought to recolonize my forbearers, ship them "back" to Liberia (or Haiti, or, really, anywhere distant), and, having secured incalculable economic boon, be rid of moral twinge.[27]

Such contradiction is precisely the force that renders violence both normal and invisible. It is an appendage of false virtue that proselytizes the demand to replicate perverted Truths in the name of equally perverted values. Indeed, the same colonial logic that compels its own (very literal) replication through civilization, colonization, and development seduces its evangelists with the hubris of divine intervention. And with the lethal blindness to the incommensurability of rules with laws.

It is thus, shrouded by the fortitude of morality, that the reflex to contradict very human-made problems is deified—and absolved—in the name of ostensible imperatives. It is thus, for instance, that, having slashed big jagged lines through bodies and space, democracy is exalted in the name of "freedom"; it is thus that, having inflected lethal allegiance to Christianity and commerce, capital and color, humanitarianism is exalted in the name of "goodness"; and it is thus that, having enshrined the world in the prison of hierarchy, human rights are exalted in the name of "equality." And, in colonial logic, nothing could possibly be wrong with freedom, goodness, or equality (thus nothing could possibly be wrong with democracy, humanitarianism, or human rights).

These are the wardens of the geography of imagination. They are the seemingly unassailable values that in fact sanction violence in their willful refusal to consider whose freedom? whose goodness? whose equality? (much less which democracy? which humanity? which rights?).

But there is another false virtue, righteousness, that secures the stranglehold of toxic solidarity. Indeed it is righteousness that renders the violence of colonial goodness, freedom, and equality invisible. And it is righteousness that fuels pernicious illusions of dissent. For righteousness is the antidote to symptoms. It is the driving force in crusades to modify policy, eventually (and grudgingly) to grant freedoms, to legislate the public chopping, and breaking, and hanging of bodies.

In the aftermath of transatlantic history, righteousness champions the dual facades of benevolence and inevitability; it is the name in which superficial modifications placate, then smother the imagination of any other way of being. In the name of righteousness, imagination is gerrymandered, confined to the Sisyphean project of ameliorating (rather than obliterating) the pernicious collective illusion of Reality dictated by colonial logic. And, handmaiden to an impotent imagination, righteousness is deified as avenger of visible violence.

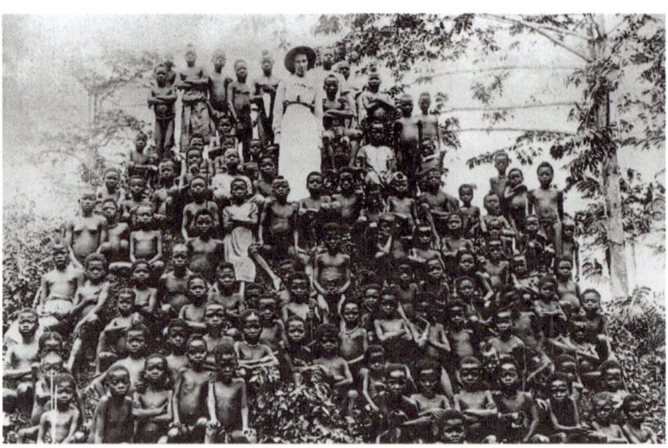

Alice Seeley Harris in Central Africa

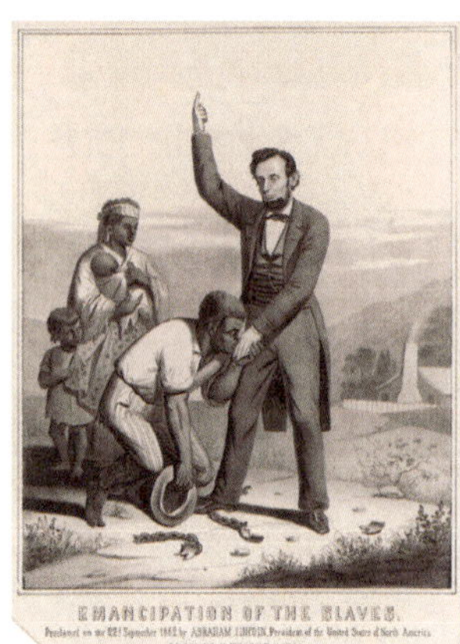

The truth, though, is that only certain violences are visible. To see that, one must see more than just Nsala. One must, among other things, see what his photographer could not: the violence of her own righteousness, of her refusal to recognize cause. One must see the illusive anatomy of the colonial gaze—the seamless choreography of complicity and imagination, and the web of illusions they coagulate in their wake.

But that is not all. To see in his dismembered encounter not only *that* something is wrong, but *which* something is wrong, one must look not just for Nsala but also for his daughter. One must look beyond symptoms of dismemberment for cause, for the "facts" and "virtues" that propel the world of lines. One must look for malevolent rules masquerading as law and see that "the extent to which technical legalisms are used to obfuscate the human motivations that generate [any] justice system is the real extent to which we as human beings are disenfranchised."[28]

And therein lies the sacred potential of contradiction: to expose rather than veil human motivations. Unlike righteous indignation, it is not, at once, a call to arms. It is, rather, a rupture in the geography of imagination, a cold trembling effort to see that which was—and is—quite literally outside the frame of view in colonial logic, to see not only how-things-came-to-be, but what else also is, was, and could be. To see thus is not only to see from both sides of the veil, but also to see the dead. And, in so doing, to grant to the disremembered and the dislocated the dignity of being lost.

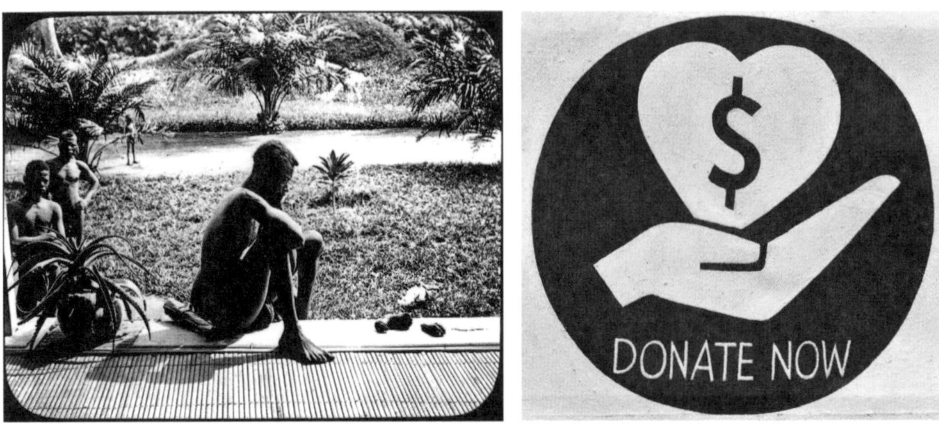

Contradict: Nsala's Daughter

6. To Create

The thing about ghosts is they cannot be unseen. No, when they take up residence, they come to stay. And they are unruly, willfully indifferent to propriety. That is, after all, the whole point of hauntings, to interrupt the illusion of reality with the demand for something else.

What precisely that something else is depends on one's ghost. Mine being Nsala's daughter, my something else hinges on matters of time, and space, and being. These, her severed possibilities, are the forces that lure me over the brink of the invisible. But, even as I decompose these matters with vigilance, I do not profess to be the sole proprietor of any revelations they may yield.

On the contrary, what I have learned from Nsala and his daughter, what I have learned from my own light-skinned, long-locked body, is that the motive of proprietorship is uniformity, and the invariable outcome of uniformity is extinction. That is to say that any system of being that sprawls beyond the nucleus of its willing adherents must, to fulfill its own logic, annihilate everyone, and everywhere, and everything else, whether through visible or invisible violence.

Extinction being the antithesis of my aim, I stake my claim no further than my own imagination. For I am a willing adherent of imagination. Not the imagination gerrymandered by the geography of complicity, but the imagination that enables us to see what once was or could have been, what isn't but still could be. The imagination, that is, to take deathly seriously the question, *What if to see is not to believe but rather to create?*

Of course, to create is no small task. It was no small task for the fragrant strangers who created Congo out of Yira land; it was no small task for those who conjured the hierarchic matrix of value and viability that suffocates the globe. And it is no small task for those who refuse systems of normalized violence and set out to exist otherwise. It is, truly, no small task. Yet it is, in my eyes, quite literally a matter of life or death. For every father's daughters, for every mother's sons whose bodies and beings are mutilated in the name of security, progress, and peace, it is a matter of life or death.

I realize that the fact of urgency, while undeniable, still does not make of creation a small task. I realize, too, that there is, by definition, no universal formula—universality and formulae being the driving engines of colonial logic. Yet, despite the many probabilities of failure, in my quest to restore to my infinite Black boys that which was lost, I choose to take the question deathly seriously. *What if to see is indeed not to believe but rather to create?* In response, I imagine, ferociously, beyond systems of sanctioned violence. I flex my rage. I unravel. And so on.

But what I have learned from decomposing the colonial gaze is that to actually inhabit a world outside the gravitational forcefield of replication and contradiction requires more than analysis or rage. It requires, first, a certain willingness to participate in the "consecration of sacrilege"—to participate, that is, in the "willing transgression of a line, which takes one into new awareness, a secret, lonely, and tabooed world."[1] Like so many lines, the borders of consecrated sacrilege expose traces of sanctioned violence not as credible proof of the-way-things-are but rather as the predictable outcome of wretched choices.

The act of transgression, then, is to actively exist otherwise. And transgression, for me, begins with naming. Indeed, inhabiting a world outside the gravitational forcefield of replication and contradiction requires a different vocabulary. To see—much less to be—outside the world of lines requires language with which to name the invisible and thus dispel the illusion that it does not or cannot exist.

And so, to create, I turn to language. I turn to language because it is one custodian of the capacity to imagine. With it I aspire to probe possibilities, to keep memories. But I do not aspire to proclaim truths. No, I refuse, willfully, either to replicate or to contradict colonial hegemonies of knowing, to add prescriptions and arguments to the shrine of universality and formulae. Instead, the meanings I mine from language are maps of possibility; they are a tiny handful among a vast expanse of ways of seeing and being that exist beyond the murderous lines of colonial logic.

But while the meanings I mine from language do not yield to the false idolatry of singular Truth, they do have roots. Their antecedent is a worldview in which to name is to bring into existence, to manifest, to create; a worldview in which names are sacred and hold power. So I begin with names. More precisely, I begin with nouns, those pillars of imagination that "establish the intellectual and political horizon of that which is sayable, credible, legitimate, or realistic and, by implication, of that which is unsayable, incredible, illegitimate, or unrealistic."[2] And, because the object of creation is, for me, a world in which Nsala's daughter could be whole, my nouns, necessarily, follow severed possibilities of time, and space, and being.

EJO LOBI

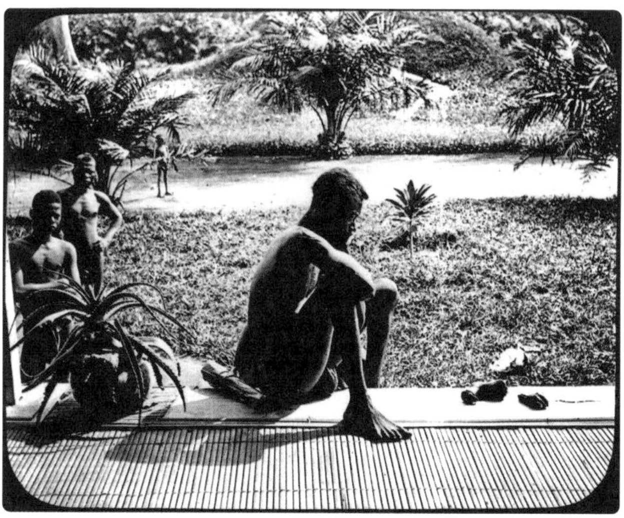

Nsala of Wala with the severed hand and foot of his five-year-old daughter, murdered by Anglo-Belgian India Rubber Company militia

Technically speaking neither Nsala nor his daughter passed through the door of no return. Their bodies were never martialed through a sordid portal of shit and stone, not incarcerated in transatlantic vessels, not branded for auction. And yet they experienced a rupture no less final, no less complete. Like their kin-turned-cargo, they, too, were martialed through ports of blood and bone, enslaved by transatlantic glut, shackled by lethal quotas. Only, like so many violences, the portals and prisons of their dismembering were—and are—invisible.

Better said, the portals and prisons of their dismembering are invisible to the unhaunted eye. Nsala's photographic afterlife is proof enough of that: his transformation into emblem and cause célèbre of the toxic solidarity of State attests, if nothing else, to the blinding power of visible violence.

But to the haunted eye his photograph tells a different story. It is still, clearly, a story of rupture. And violence. But it is not solely, not even primarily, rupture and violence perpetrated against bodies. Obviously the story is told through bodies: Nsala's presence, his daughter's (mostly) absence, his lookers-on, his machine wielding looker-at. But, to the haunted eye, the subject of this photograph is neither Nsala nor his daughter.

It is, instead, a door of no return. Not a physical door, not the stuff of shit and stone, but still a portal through which everything was—and is—re-created by the colonial gaze.

This is not a metaphor for the dismemberment of Nsala's daughter. It is, rather, a reckoning of what, besides bodies, was martialed to extinction in the name of Christianity and commerce, capital and color. Like any encounter with the dead, it is a demand to see the many and varied victims of colonial logic. And, in Nsala's case, the victims include not just his daughter but also the very notion of time.

Indeed, whatever its author's intent, this is, quite literally, a photograph of the end of time as Nsala knew it. To the haunted eye, it is a photograph of time itself being martialed through the door of no return; of time—in the clutches of that which transformed bodies into chattel—being transformed into the dictator, metric, and false synonym of progress.

Akin to the matriarch of Yira land's tale of fragrant strangers, this image is both proof and consequence of time, like space, being coerced into a cunning lethal line. It is a blueprint of the logic—and the exigencies—of a system in which the future, forever yet to come, reigns tyrant, commanding, in the perpetual present, blind allegiance to the cardinal pillars of complicity; of a system in which faith, commerce, law, and science compel indentured servitude with the lure of future reward (whether paradise, prosperity, power, or perpetual life).

It is, too, a blueprint of the logic—and the exigencies—of a system in which output, however irrelevant to the sustenance of life, is the sole determinant of survival; in which Nsala, oblivious and disloyal to the geography of complicity, failed to labor in time with progress (to procure a substance irrelevant to the sustenance of life), and is thus denied survival as a matter of "law."

The great and morbid irony of this photograph is the ambiguous absence of the dead girl. In one view, traces of her presence serve as evidence of the need for reform. But that is in the eyes of those who never saw her whole; in eyes offended by the collateral damage of output, but blind to the tyranny—much less the fallacy—of progress. Blind, that is, to the fact that progress in the world of lines is, uniformly and exclusively, premised on death. Not death by virtue of time (an actual law of nature) but death by virtue of coerced labor (the golden rule of colonial logic). And therein lies the fallacy of progress: the willful conflation of the inevitability of the former with evitability of the latter in the delusional crusade for future reward.

It is, indeed, a great and morbid irony that traces of the dead girl's presence overshadow the absolute predictability of her absence and thus inspire reform (rather than rejection) of the colonial dictum of progress. But this is decidedly not a question of the past, of a bygone era in which Nsala and his accomplices walked this earth. Nor is it a question of any particular place. It is, instead, a question of how we choose to see.

And of that Nsala is a haunting barometer. To see his image as evidence of a bodily crime is itself a violence far more destructive than the blows that rent his daughter limb from limb. To see it thus is to overlook the four very intact people in plain view, who could—and did—quite literally see her whole. And to overlook them is to overlook their view of the world, in which dismemberment is not inevitable. And to overlook their view of the world is to disremember that which exists outside the world of lines and its tyrannical dictums of progress.

Of course, it is a mighty challenge to see their view of the world. For to see, as did Nsala and his lookers-on, a world in which his daughter could be whole, is to re-member that which exists outside the lines of progress.[3] This is not to conjure, much less endeavor to inhabit, an idyllic past; it is not to ascribe undue virtue to the dead. No, to re-member is not to indulge fantasy. It is, rather, to reckon, rigorously, with that which was—and is—disremembered by colonial logic. And that includes not just bodies, but also the very notion of time.

Indeed, save for the colonial rupture, Nsala would have bequeathed to his daughter a different place and a different time. It would not have been Congo, the origin of which was the gluttonous delusion of fragrant strangers (*in the beginning was the word and the word was with man . . .*). It would have been a different place, birthed by Nyamuhanga, bequeathed from father to daughter, from mother to son with a different story.

But, like so many violences, that story has been disremembered. And, as much as I would give to re-member it, I would not dare approximate. What I do know is this: birth stories, by definition, are stories in a middle. They commemorate a moment (however protracted) of emergence that is at once a culmination of one form of gestation and the advent of others. They commemorate a process that is the result of itself—an emergence of a body from a body that itself emerged from a body that emerged from a body. In this sense they are embedded in lineage and ancestry. And yet birth stories, like births themselves, mark a beginning. A beginning in a middle. A beginning that comes from what was and leads to what might be. They are, by definition, a story—and a proof—of ancestored possibility.

And, while the particulars of Nyamuhanga's story have been disremembered, the prospect of ancestored possibility has not been fully extinguished. Wherever possible it has been legislated out of practice. But, like every ghost, it lingers. In language, for instance. In words like *ejo* and *lobi*—the one Kinyarwanda, the other Lingala—which convey, in a single term, a concept segregated by the world of lines into "yesterday" and "tomorrow."

For their disloyalty to the vocabulary of progress these (like so many) languages are branded "poor," held in contempt, replaced, and repressed by the mandates of Christianity and commerce, capital and color. And yet—or perhaps therefore—they hold precious clues to that which exists outside the lines of progress.

Indeed, ejo and lobi are pillars of a worldview that refuses to cleave temporality into linear trajectories of "past" and "future." To encompass, in a word, the great expanse of yesterday and tomorrow is to insist that we are already—and always—living in both; that every moment exists in yesterday's tomorrow *and* in tomorrow's yesterday. It is to see that every moment, like every action, is both ancestor and possibility, both effect and cause.

Given the precarious fate of that which exists outside the lines of progress, I cling ferociously to ejo lobi.[4] The meaning I extract may well surpass its colloquial, even poetic jurisdiction. But I turn to language not to confine but to imagine, to create.

Mining ejo lobi has taught me that to see—much less to create—a world in which dismemberment is not inevitable has everything to do with how we choose to understand and occupy time. Like so many unwilling prisoners of colonial logic, I have long understood that time measured in terms of output inevitably yields extinction. The consecrated sacrilege of ejo lobi is the reminder that there are other ways to measure time; that the line so urgently in need of transgression is the one created by gluttonous delusions of the dictums of progress.

Thus, like the door of no return, ejo lobi is a portal of sorts. It is an antidote to colonial logic in which cause is in the custody of the past, and effect is unaccountable because its overlord, the future, is always yet-to-come. It is a blueprint of the logic—and the exigencies—of a worldview in which every action is both ancestor and possibility, both effect and cause. It is, therefore, also a blueprint of the logic—and the exigencies—of the choices that do and do not sustain life.

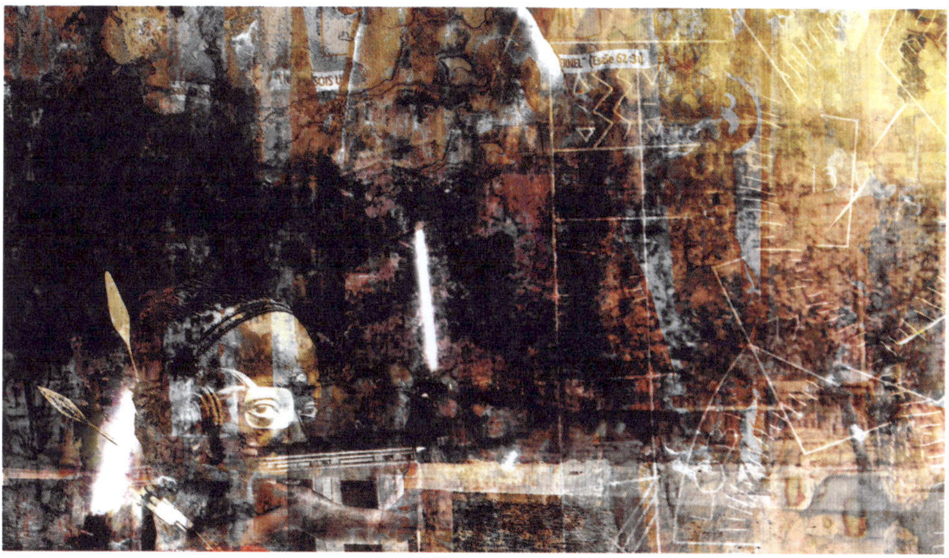

Ejo Lobi

FROM

Technically speaking, I did not pass through the door of no return any more than Nsala or his daughter did. I am, however, a product of those who did. I do not know who, or where, or when their bodies were martialed through which sordid portal of shit and stone, incarcerated in transatlantic vessel, branded for auction. But I do know why.

Even before I learned to see the dead I could see the logic that perverts bodies into property, that perverts time into overseer of progress, that, in pursuit of dominion, is blind to all but Christianity and commerce, capital and color. I could see that logic in my own mutilated family tree, whose limbs are severed two rungs shy of Louisa White; I could see it in my inherited memories of Mrs. Boudreaux; in the parable of my own improbability.

I could see, too, that just as this logic severs past from future, it severs origin from place. Indeed, for those bisected by the defining lines of color and state, identity is not measured in terms of space but in terms of function. In this sense it matters little that I intercepted the memories of my great-grandma Louisa in Plaquemine, Louisiana, for she was only there by virtue of her great-grandma whoever-she-was's function.

This is why, before I learned to see the dead, I could not, with dignity, say where I was from. I could not claim to be from Plaquemine, Louisiana, any more than I could claim to be from Yira land. That is to say, I could not trace my being any further in space than the belly of a slave ship and a capitalist state.

Yet I was not immune to the lure of belonging. To the contrary, I went great lengths to conjure for myself a link to space that might conquer diasporic alienation, that might resolve the question of origin with ancestral roots. Or at least with a place to claim. In this pursuit I marched my light-skinned, long-locked body to many a door of no return; I touched and smelled the sordid portals; I gorged myself on every trace of proof of what once was—every way of being, seeing, saying, praying, knowing, healing, making, unmaking, giving, taking, birthing, flying. I devoured every story, song, gesture, taste, touch, sight, smell; I did all within my power to enshrine in flesh and bone a fortress of language, names, and culture. And it was, for me, a certain balm.

But then I learned to see the dead. And seeing the dead cost me every last scrap of the illusion of belonging. With time I have come to see that this was both an excruciating and a liberating loss. It wrenched from me any hope that the question of origin could be resolved by virtue of locating ancestral bodies in space. It also taught me to see the precious possibility that the question of origin is not (at least not only, or even primarily) a matter of where but also a matter of what.

Thus, seeing the dead redeemed for me the question of origin. Recast it not as a quest to locate bodies in space but to locate bodies of knowledge. Like everything about the dead, this is not a matter of fantasy or indulgence, not a

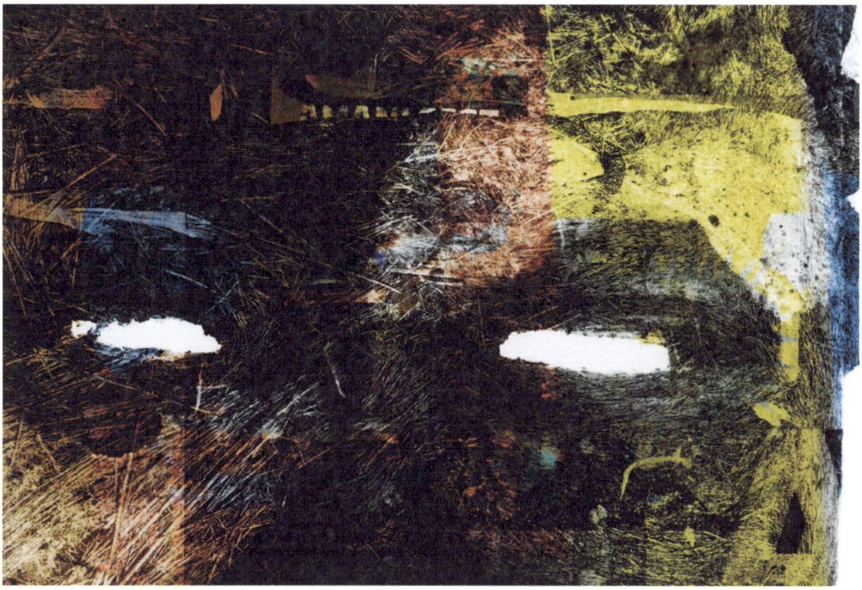

From

matter of adopting a veneer of ancient or exotic wisdom. It is, rather, a matter of re-membering practices of knowing even as they have been purged from place.

In this sense it makes a world of difference that I intercepted my great-grandma Louisa's memories in Plaquemine, Louisiana. It makes a world of difference that despite her great-grandma whoever-she-was's function, there in the land of cotton and cane Louisa Johnson Harris Wright White threw Mrs. Boudreaux's cabbage in the trash. And grew her own. Always in front of the children.

It makes a world of difference because it is a reminder of ways, big and small, to re-member that which exists outside colonial logic. Wherever one happens to be (and why ever one happens to be there). For her part, Great-Grandma Louisa refused to disremember the kind of labor that sustains life. Even as that very labor was perverted all around her by Christianity and commerce, capital and color; even as it was weaponized in veneration of transatlantic glut, she refused to accept the tyrannical dictums of progress as her only possibility.

She was, clearly, not exempt from the exigencies of progress—she was, after all, a Black woman in the southern United States. But even as she was assaulted by the world of lines, she never lost sight of its architecture. She understood, for instance, that the opposite of progress is not stagnation, not the brutal primitive destitution conjured by colonial logic to insure allegiance to its fallacies. No, in her view of the world, the opposite of progress was—and is—survival. Not because she was from any particular place, but because she was rooted in a particular body of knowledge.

So she threw Mrs. Boudreaux's cabbage in the trash. And grew her own.

Refusing Mrs. Boudreaux's charity was not an act of spite (indeed, Great-Grandma Louisa thanked Mrs. Boudreaux and left her none the wiser). It was, rather, an act of survival. It was a reminder to herself—and to her children's children—that, without vigilance, the illusion of beneficence, like any form of toxic solidarity, would imprison her not only in Mrs. Boudreaux's but also in her own imagination. It was a reminder that, without vigilance, she would learn dependence on the very system that turned her kin to cargo.

In point of fact, Great-Grandma Louisa never physically set foot outside the world of lines. Unlike the matriarchs of Yira land, she could not point to any particular piece of earth that shaped her view of the world. And yet she remembered. And, in so doing, she bequeathed a blueprint of the logic—and the exigencies—of life exempt from the tyrannical dictums of progress, of what still could be.

This blueprint is the closest thing I have to a point of origin. It does nothing to resolve the question of space, and in that sense it does not tell me where I am from. But it solves the problem anyway. It permits me to point, with certainty, to a body of knowledge that shapes my view of the world.

In my quest to restore to my infinite Black boys that which was lost I stumbled on the need to name whatever-it-is Great-Grandma Louisa bequeathed. And I landed on "from." For "from" is the best word I can find to call that which harbors the ghosts of origin in the aftermath of transatlantic history; for that which was purged from place by jagged and mendacious lines; for the ways of knowing that were martialed to extinction by colonial logic and yet that persist.

Thus, in complement to its utility as measure of time and space, I have come to think of "from" as a noun, as a thing one has. Bisected by the defining lines of color and state, my from is a coagulation of remnants, accumulated fragments of knowing—the people, places, and things—that remain in the wake of visible violence. But, like Nsala's daughter's severed limbs, my from, as I conceive it, also harbors invisible victims. It harbors, in particular, what once was or could have been, what isn't but still could be. In this sense, a from is a demand to remember that the question of origin is not a matter of earth, not even of bloodlines, but of the bodies of knowledge we do (or do not) see as our blueprint of being.

I know what I do about Great-Grandma Louisa in part because blood is more reliable than boxes in matters of inheritance. But also because, before she died, she wrote a letter. Not to me per se, but to ward off disremembering. And though I never met her, this letter is a cardinal pillar of my from. Not so much for what it says in word (it is a record of three dreams) but for the fact that it made its way into my hands. And for what that fact re-members, for the possibilities it ancestors, and for the precious demand it puts on me to see the dead—wherever I happen to be.

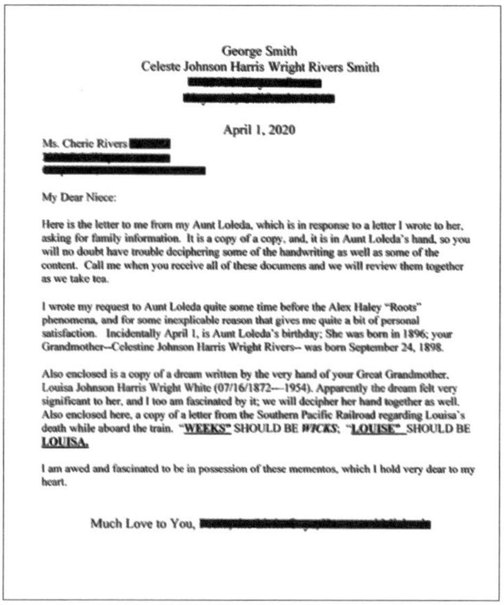

George Smith
Celeste Johnson Harris Wright Rivers Smith

April 1, 2020

Ms. Cherie Rivers

My Dear Niece:

Here is the letter to me from my Aunt Loleda, which is in response to a letter I wrote to her, asking for family information. It is a copy of a copy, and, it is in Aunt Loleda's hand, so you will no doubt have trouble deciphering some of the handwriting as well as some of the content. Call me when you receive all of these documens and we will review them together as we take tea.

I wrote my request to Aunt Loleda quite some time before the Alex Haley "Roots" phenomena, and for some inexplicable reason that gives me quite a bit of personal satisfaction. Incidentally April 1, is Aunt Loleda's birthday; She was born in 1896; your Grandmother--Celestine Johnson Harris Wright Rivers-- was born September 24, 1898.

Also enclosed is a copy of a dream written by the very hand of your Great Grandmother, Louisa Johnson Harris Wright White (07/16/1872—1954). Apparently the dream felt very significant to her, and I too am fascinated by it; we will decipher her hand together as well. Also enclosed here, a copy of a letter from the Southern Pacific Railroad regarding Louisa's death while aboard the train. "**WEEKS**" SHOULD BE ***WICKS***; "**LOUISE**" SHOULD BE **LOUISA.**

I am awed and fascinated to be in possession of these mementos, which I hold very dear to my heart.

Much Love to You,

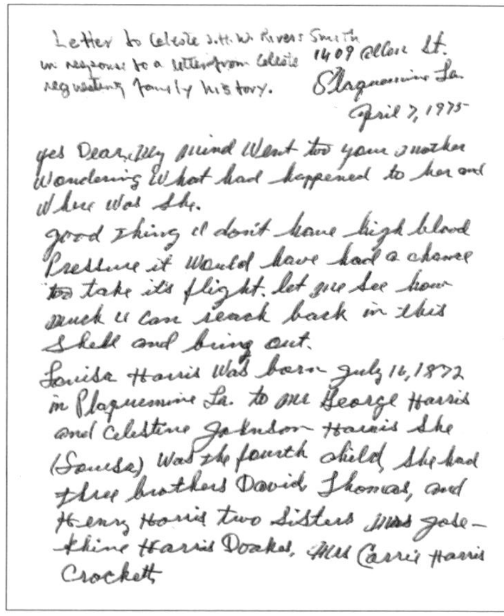

Letter to Celeste J.H.W. Rivers Smith
in response to a letter from Celeste
requesting family history.

1409 Allen St.
Plaquemine La.
April 7, 1975

yes Dear, My mind Went too your mother Wondering What had happened to her and Where Was She.
good thing I dont have high blood Pressure it Would have had a chance too take it's flight. let me See how much I can reach back in this Shell and bring out.
Louisa Harris Was born July 16, 1872 in Plaquemine La. to Mr George Harris and Celestine Johnson Harris She (Louisa) Was the fourth child, She had three brothers David Thomas, and Henry Harris two Sisters Mrs Josephine Harris Doakes, Mrs Carrie Harris Crockett

ORPHANED WONDERING

For the dead to be seen, either they or their seer must pass, in reverse, through the door of no return. Either they or their seer must confront the portal through which everything was—and is—re-created in colonial logic. And then transgress it. There are, of course, as many ways to transgress as there are ghosts. One of them is to decompose the cardinal pillars on which colonial logic stands.

This is, in part, a project of seeing the formula that sustains the world of lines. For though each pillar—faith, commerce, law, and science—has its own particulars, they share a common blueprint: they each coerce a foundational fallacy into Truth; they are each indentured to a false idol; they each demand and consecrate a lethal process in the name of future reward.

Faith, for its part, rests squarely on the delusion that man, like God, has the right (both the power and the prerogative, that is) to create the world in his own image. In homage to this fallacy, human will has been coerced into the custodian of the divine, and faith, in the world of lines, has indentured itself to the idol of man. Not any man, of course, not Nsala and certainly not his daughter, for they, like their kin-turned-cargo, were—and are—not recognized as such. Instead faith serves as shield and spur for those who would re-create the world in their own image. And while their crusades, their righteousness, their charity are cause of certain death for Nsala and his daughter, their reward, in the world of lines, is promise of paradise.

Commerce has as foundational fallacy the willful conflation of progress with life. In adulation of the false idol of surplus, commerce coerces survival into glut, perverts the very real need for material sustenance into the frenzied accumulation of excess. Its process, coerced labor, drives bodies and machines through time and space so haunted by fear that the promise of future prosperity is worth any and every cost. Thus Nsala's daughter, whose death is inevitable in the pursuit of capital, is coerced into a problem of policy so as not to interfere with the business of life.

The foundational fallacy of law is the hallowing of rules. It is the willful conflation of natural with manmade truths. Like faith, it rests on the delusion that man has the omnipotent right, both the power and the prerogative, to command the world. Its idol, order, demands conformity above all else.[5] And at all cost. In exchange is the promise of power. But the disorderly, however they are deemed, are, without fail, condemned—by "law"—to domination and death.[6]

Though perhaps more elusive, science, too, rests on a fallacy. It is the delusion that the world is the sum of singular—and thus objective—Truth. And in the name of singular, objective Truth, the science of the world of lines coerces certain knowledge into fact. The rest it discards as fiction. Thus disguised as gatekeeper of the-one-and-only-Truth, science peddles the illusion that there is only one way to see. And that seeing thus is, simply, Reality, to be believed at all cost. In this way science ordains itself overlord of what and how we know, supreme deity of a (tyrannical) hierarchy of thought. From this almighty throne it worships at the shrine of uniformity, commanding obedience to its omnipotence in the perpetual pursuit to prolong life.

This is, in short, the blueprint of the world of lines, the fallacies, idols, demands, and promises that compose the colonial gaze. There are, of course, more details, more nuances of time and place. The point, though, is that every time and every place that was—and is—re-created in colonial logic rests on the pillars of faith, commerce, law, and science. And that, in addition to fallacies, idols, processes, and promises, these pillars also take hostages.

Indeed, the world of lines is premised on the extinction of everyone, and everywhere, and everything that is oblivious, much less disloyal, to its dictums. And what it cannot extinguish it holds hostage. The hostage of faith is spirit, that unruly force whose allegiance to the divine does not bend to human interest. The hostage of commerce is awareness of the relationship between cause and effect, the immutable record of action. The hostage of law is purpose, the sacrosanct motive of choices that do—or do not—sustain life. And the hostage of science is creativity, the infinite possibilities that reside in chaos.

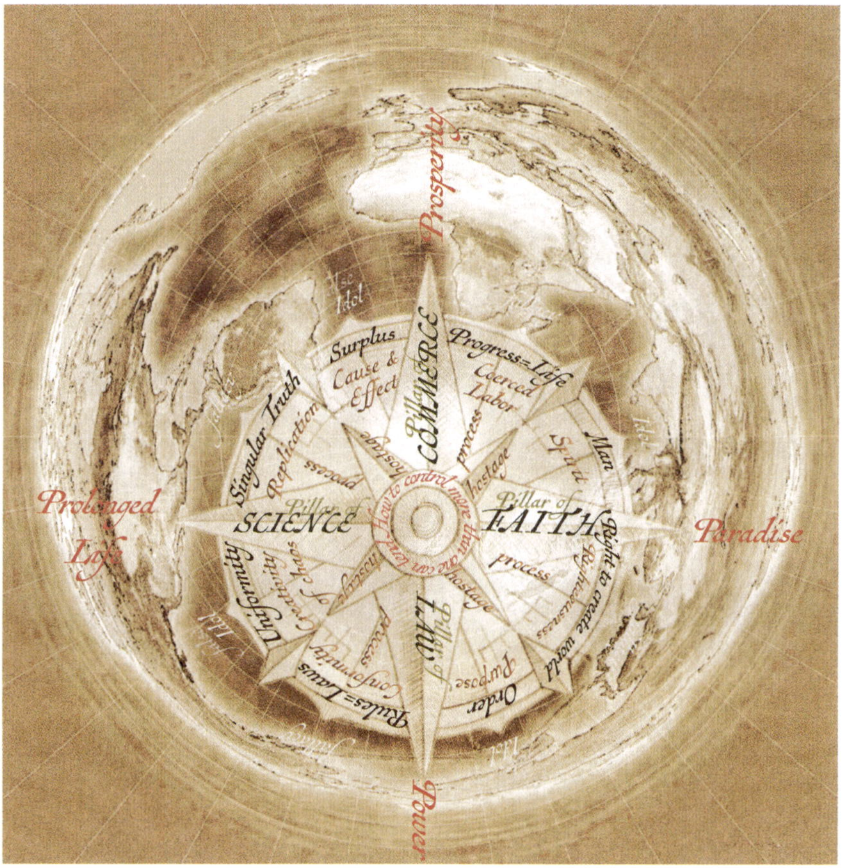

Colonial Logic

Though not entirely extinct, the hostages of colonial logic are shackled in the world of lines. They are overshadowed and confined, at best afforded tepid tribute but eviscerated of any real force. Their imprisonment has many consequences. Most relevant to the project of seeing the dead is that it leaves orphans in its wake. Including wonder. The feral will, that is, to wonder, with vigilance, about everyone, and everywhere, and everything thing that is oblivious, better yet less disloyal, to colonial logic.

This is the sort of wonder that is orphaned by the dictums of Christianity and commerce, capital and color. It is, too, the sort of wonder that leads to the door through which either ghosts or their seers must pass; the sort of wonder that recalibrates the geography of imagination with unruly questions about the dead. Like: What are the cardinal pillars of a worldview that actually sustains life?

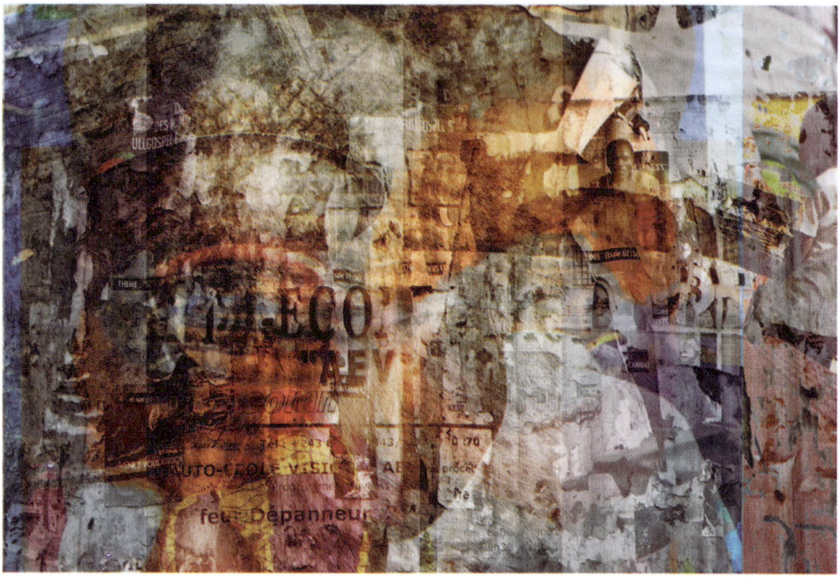

Orphane
Wonderir

Of course there are as many answers as there are ghosts. And that is precisely the power of orphaned wondering: it does not yield universal Truth. Nor can it, for it is the product of the very hostages—spirit, the ability to perceive cause and effect, purpose, and creative chaos—that negate the deadly delusion that universality can sustain life (much less yield security or peace). Indeed orphaned wondering is, instead, an antidote to universality and formulae, to the driving engines of colonial logic. It is the precious chaos from which to imagine new possibilities; a portal to what still could be.

Haunted by Nsala's daughter, by the parable of my own improbability, I wonder about orphans of time, and space, and being. I wonder about the geographies of spirit and of purpose, about what relationship between cause and effect permits Nsala's daughter to be whole. To wonder thus is to transgress, is to interrupt the illusion of reality with the possibility of something else. To consecrate that possibility, I seek nouns for the unnameable to dispel the illusion that it does not or cannot exist. And I take deathly seriously the question, *If to see is not to believe but rather to create, then how and who and where and what and why do I choose to see?*

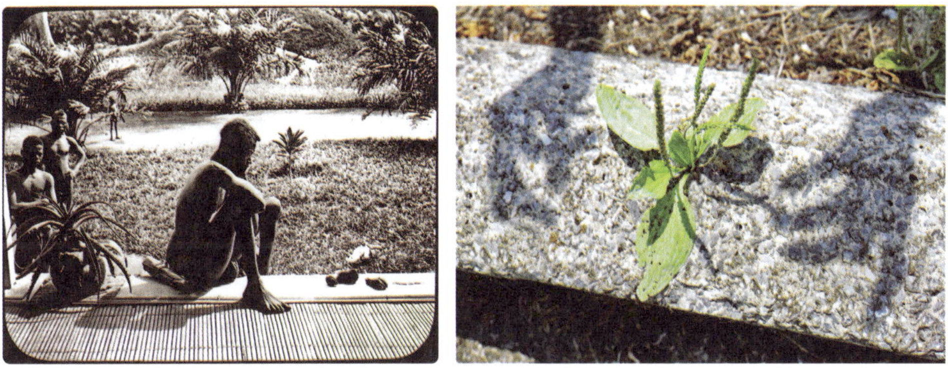

Create: Nsala's Daughter

7. To Love Nsala's Daughter

According to the terms of our contract, I was not supposed to pass, in reverse, through the door of no return. Nor was I supposed to unravel, much less to learn to see the dead. I was, rather, supposed to do my part of a collaborative educational and/or creative partnership centering on the photographs of a famed British missionary, to orchestrate a series of workshops and activities, to issue a final report. At best to usher a motley band of artists, educators, civil society leaders to the brink of revolution. I was, in effect, supposed to ignoble the prospect of decolonizing an archive with diverse local (and well-credentialed) voices.

But then a dead girl walked in with my sons. And with them came the demand that I do better. With them came the demand to see the many wounds—wounds gauged into bodies in the name of progress, wounds gauged into landscapes in the name of development, wounds gauged into economies in the name of freedom . . . With them came the demand to see all the wounds that are sanctioned by systems of normalized violence.

As a woman of African descent these wounds were never unfamiliar to me. They are, after all, the overlords that condition my perception of time, and space, and being; they are the authors of the blueprint of my own improbability. But seeing the dead forces me to see them differently.

More to the point, seeing the dead forces me to see in them the depth of my own complicity in colonial logic. It forces me to see that my place in systems of normalized violence is measured not only, or even primarily, in terms of effect but in terms of cause. That even as my very being is target of past and present controversy, I am not absolved of the violences I myself perpetrate.

Some of them are visible. I depend, for instance, on the fruits of Christianity and commerce, capital and color, and in this sense the material reality of my sustenance sprawls far beyond my nucleus of willing adherents. That is, quite literally, a cause of death. And no amount of rage or absolution can ever make it otherwise.

Like every prisoner of the world of lines, I am guilty, too, of invisible violences. Chief among them is the failure to transgress as often as I might. Sometimes for fear of invisibility, sometimes for exhaustion from the burden of reflecting history, sometimes for fury at my lot in the prison of perception. Yet whatever justification these motives may supply, every failure to transgress affirms my complicity in sustaining the colonial gaze.

Complicity being antithetical to my aim, seeing the dead prevents me, with dignity, from leading anyone to the brink of revolution. It prevents me, with dignity, from putting my light-skinned, long-locked body to the service of anything akin to colonial redemption by metaphor. Because colonial redemption is perfectly incommensurate with metaphor. And no amount of hope or semblance can ever make it otherwise.

Thus I, for one, can no longer ignore the contradictions inbred in the prospect of decolonizing any institution in the world of lines. Including archives. And yet I cling, with feral will, to the possibilities they harbor to grant to the disremembered the dignity of being lost. Not by virtue of metaphor but by virtue of the very real labor of re-membering, of transgressing the many lines between the lethal illusion of Reality and what still could be.

NSALA'S DAUGHTER

It is no secret that, in my view of the world, that which needs re-membering is Nsala's daughter. And not by metaphor. Obviously no one will ever again meet her in the flesh; obviously every earthly possibility she might have ancestored is extinct. In that sense she is, of course, a symbol. But the labor of re-membering her is very, very real.

The trick, though, is that the only way to re-member Nsala's daughter is to dismember the world that renders her death inevitable. This begins with the ability to see her. To see, in each and every encounter, the ghosts of our choices; to see who and where and what was—and is—dismembered to fulfill the whims of fragrant strangers everywhere.

In a world erupting in flames, bullets, and bombs I need not point out that the ghosts of our choices are many. They are human and material, natural and divine. And all of them are haunted by Nsala's daughter. For she was—and is—not just a forgotten five-year-old girl in the heart of a place some now call Congo. She is an embodied barometer of cause and effect. In this sense, Nsala's daughter is a demand to measure desire against the question of just how many ounces of rubber, just how many ounces of anything, justify slaughter.

But that is not all; Nsala's daughter is more than that. Indeed she is an embodied barometer of all that is held hostage by colonial logic. She is a measure of spirit, a demand to question the sanctity of any faith in league with commerce. She is a measure of purpose, a demand to question the incestuous substitution of need with want. Though perhaps more elusive, she is, too, a measure of the creativity of chaos, a scathing reminder that eliminating possibilities of space and time also eliminates the possibility of being.

Nsala's daughter is all this and more. And yet there is no record of her name. That is, indeed, a great and morbid irony. It is product and proof of colonial logic, for without a name, she does not exist. Just as her body cannot be whole in the world of Christianity and commerce, capital and color, without a name, any possibility she harbors is held hostage. And thus disremembered, she cannot serve as counterpoint to the lethal world of lines.

Despite my reverence for the catalytic power of nouns, I realize it would be ridiculous to conjure for her a name. So I re-member her otherwise. I re-member her in every effort, big or small, to embody that which is orphaned by colonial logic. I re-member her in every effort, big or small, to ancestor possibilities calibrated to purpose, to see beyond the limits of faith the many traces of spirit, to actively exist otherwise in time and space. In short, I re-member her as a profoundly active verb. And it is in this sense that I, for one, aspire to be Nsala's daughter.

My final—and most sacred—duty to Nsala is to decompose the notion of love. For it is one thing to see his daughter, but it is another thing entirely to love her. Indeed, to see her is to fix our eyes on possibilities rendered invisible by systems of normalized violence. But though it is a mighty struggle, to see, alone, does nothing to re-member her.

To love her does. To love her is to venture over the brink of invisible possibility and take up permanent residence in what still could be. It is to pledge feral-willed allegiance to the many possibilities orphaned by colonial logic. This is clearly no small task. Yet love is the only way I know to transgress the many lethal lines dividing what is from what still could be. It is a hallowed door of no return. And thus it is sacred.

But make no mistake, love in the logic of decomposing is not patient, not kind.[1] Love is fierce. It may well be the only force powerful enough to dismember the world of lines. And it leaves nothing intact. Because love in the logic of decomposing is a perpetual transgression.

Indeed love is the most sacred possibility of intelligent rage. It is the source of the cold trembling knowledge that dismemberment is never partial. That it was not partial for Nsala, whose worldview, like his daughter, was severed by colonial logic. It was neither partial for the matriarchs of Yira land, whose land and possibilities were annihilated by a big jagged line. Nor is it partial on the other side of the sea. Not partial for Margaret Garner and her many unnamed sisters, who sliced clean through their babies' throats to spare them from Christianity and commerce, capital and color.[2]

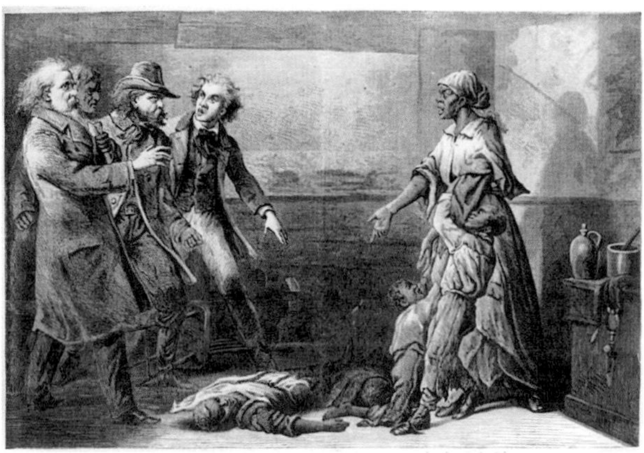

Margaret Garner, having killed her daughter rather than return her to slavery, being arrested on the Underground Railroad. She was later returned to her master and convicted of property damage.

No, dismemberment is never partial. But it is, at times, an act of love. Such was the case for Margaret Garner, who showed her children the greatest—indeed the only—love afforded by the world of lines. She absolved them of it. Nsala was denied such grace. And yet his daughter was still absolved. Though afforded different agency, Margaret Garner and Nsala have something immutable in common: they know that one way or another their children will be absolved of the world of lines, for there is no possibility for both to exist. The question is which one to dismember.

These are the stakes of love. To love the world of lines is to dismember Nsala's daughter. To love Nsala's daughter is to dismember the world of lines. Not in part, but in whole. Anything less is a willful delusion. For despite the best illusions of faith, commerce, law, and science, there is no love in the world of lines that does not dismember Nsala's daughter. And despite the best illusions of faith, commerce, law, and science, there is no place for colonial logic in a world in which she could be whole. To love her, then, is to dismember every last trace of the colonial gaze.

Of course, like every act of love, this comes at a cost. At stake are the many illusions peddled by Christianity and commerce, capital and color. Illusions of security, and progress, and peace; illusions of endless want and endless matter; illusions of righteousness and charity. At stake is every false idol—of man, and surplus, and order, and uniformity—that commands allegiance to normalized violence in promise of future reward. At stake is every myth, every image, every code generated by colonial logic.

To love Nsala's daughter is to dismember each and every one of these illusions in whole. And to replace them with something else. This is not a matter of quarantining history or driving memories to extinction. No, love in the logic of decomposing does not take hostages. It is, rather, a matter of re-membering the cardinal pillars of a worldview that can actually sustain life. And that is, in turn, a matter of re-membering the balance between what is—and is not—infinite.

In a world imploding from poison, pestilence, and plague I need not point out the material nature of the finite. Despite the best illusions of faith, commerce, law, and science, Nsala's daughter is irrefutable proof that the power of man, and surplus, and order, and uniformity is both finite and toxic.

But to anyone willing to love her, Nsala's daughter is also proof that spirit, purpose, and the creativity of chaos are infinite. This is both the precious possibility and the demand of love. For spirit, purpose, and the creativity of chaos are not all that is infinite. So is the relationship between cause and effect. Whether or not we choose to be aware of it. In this sense, to love Nsala's daughter is to refuse complicity in all its forms. It is to refuse the many very real pressures to disguise laws and history as facts of time and space, to absolve ourselves with the delusion that this-is-how-things-are (and thus that there-is-nothing-we-can-do), to absolve ourselves with the delusion that the intent of an act in any way mitigates its consequences.

Like the labor of re-membering, the labor of love is very, very real. In the logic of decomposing the colonial gaze, the labor of love is to create infinite ways, big and small, to exist outside the fortress of lines. The matriarchs of Yira land's was a labor of love; Margaret Garner's was a labor of love, as was Great-Grandma Louisa's. Each in their way did everything within their power to exist otherwise.

Mine, too, is a labor of love. Like the matriarchs of Yira land, and Margaret Garner, and Great-Grandma Louisa, I seek each and every way I can to absolve my body and my imagination from colonial logic. For decomposing the colonial gaze has taught me to see that they have bequeathed a precious inheritance to anyone who seeks the dead: the blueprint of the logic—and the exigencies—of a worldview that actually sustains life.

I see this as the precious possibility of restoring to my infinite Black boys that which was lost. And so, in honor of known and unknown matriarchs, I keep memories and refuse compromise. In their honor I discard illusions of beneficence and grow my own cabbages. In their honor I transgress as often and as wholly as I can. Always in front of the children—in front of anyone who will pay attention.

But I do not teach them to thank the proverbial Mrs. Boudreaux, much less to take her charity—for in my eyes she can no longer afford to be none the wiser. Yet nor do I teach them to despise her. Instead I teach them to see the dead, to decompose, to be ancestored possibilities of Nsala's daughter. And, in hopes that they might love—and live—despite the odds, I pray with feral will: *Oh, my heart, make of me always a woman who wonders!*

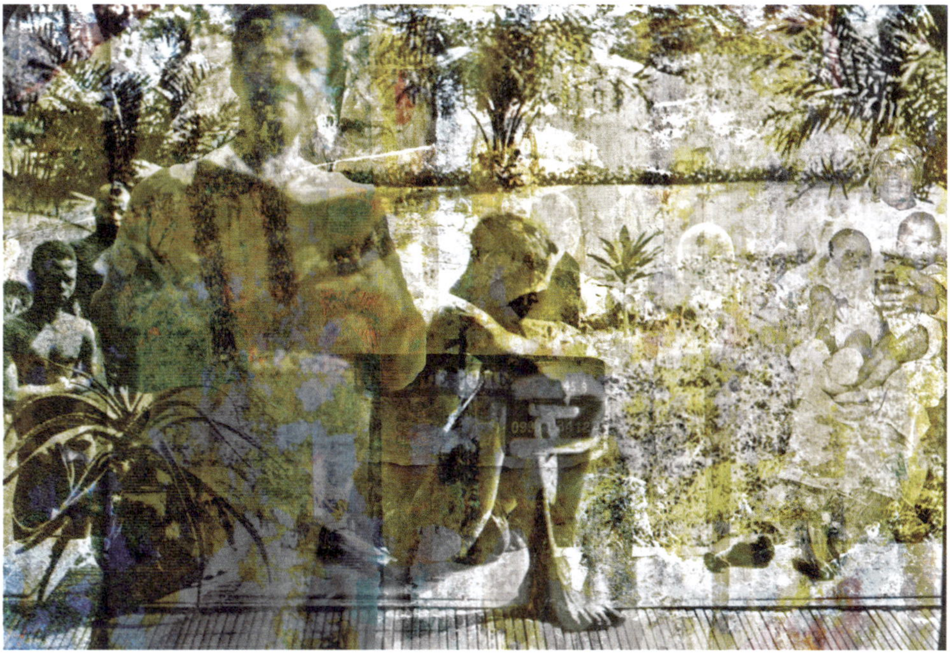

Nyamuhanga Apipawe!

Gratitude

Of all the gifts Nsala's daughter gave me, there are three I hold most dear. One is the knowledge that decomposing is a labor of love. Another is the knowledge that the hostages are not, nor will they ever be, extinct. And third is the knowledge that honoring the blueprint of a worldview that actually sustains life is a labor of gratitude. For these and all her other gifts I am fiercely grateful.

I am fiercely grateful, too, to the many beings—dead and living, human and more-than-human—whose energies enabled me to give myself over to this book:

To the (perhaps unwitting) instigator of my unraveling, Katie Donnington, for penning a haunting correspondence that unleashed a world of ghosts, then weathering the storms wrought by my allegiance to them.

To the modern-day abolitionists at the Universities of Nottingham and Liverpool, for entrusting me and my accomplice to usher an archive home and, a dozen decades deferred, respond to the images that introduced "the Congo" to "the World."

To the sanctuaries, Yole!Africa and Picha, that first embraced the practice of decomposing, and to the early decomposers—in particular Sarah Mukadi, Moustache Muhanya, David Shongo Mafungwa, Bernadette Vivuya, Dorine Mokha, and Kagoma Twahirgwa—for accompanying me to the brink of visible possibility.

To Elizabeth Olson, for ushering me into a world where ghosts are welcome, and to Andrea Bohlman, for reminding me to inhabit it on my own terms.

To the National Humanities Center, for the gift of time and space to live with ghosts; to the superhuman librarians who conjured the impossible from around the globe (and with such grace!); and to my fellow 2019–20 fellows, for the countless parts they played in a year that changed me for the better.

To Elizabeth Ault, for being both a reader and an editor to whom my light-skinned, long-locked body could, with confidence, entrust this record of my haunting. To the team Benjamin Kossak, Liz Smith, and Matthew Tauch at Duke University Press, for embracing the many demands that inevitably come with ghosts. And to the anonymous readers whose time and insight shaped these pages for the better.

To the generous artisans, including Nzanzu Boboy, M. Castofas, Tushar Varma, Caroline Brogden, and Derek Gottlieb, for plying their crafts that the world might see.

To the memory-keepers of Yira land, for reminding me of what still could be; and to all who dwell in Uzuri Sanctuary for turning possibility into force of habit.

To the memory-keepers of the Rivers tribe—Aunt Celeste, Aunt Daisy, and the battalion of cousins who hold me close—for causing a precious bundle of letters to arrive in my hands. I will keep them to my dying day, and beyond.

To the many ancestors of my bones and my imagination, including Isaac Rivers and Biodun Jeyifo, who taught me how—and why—to be Nsala's daughter.

To my fellow wonderers, Natasha McCurley and Simon Rose, for nourishing my courage and my will to share these stories with the world; to Linda Williams, for receiving them with open arms; to Sherah Faulkner, for the wizardry with which she corralled them into physical form; to Fowota Mortoo, for insisting I give them voice. And to Wesley Morris, for venturing over the brink of invisible possibility and tending what still could be with tenacious care.

To the human pillars on whom I rely as I incubate imagination—Katie Mentz, for holding the *jiko* together when ghosts demand that I am elsewhere; Michael Cohen, for sparking my process of radical clarity; and Karen Rivers, for life after life of unconditional love.

To my infinite Black boys, Mokozi and Issé, for the precious gift of reverent maternal rage and for ushering a dead girl in their wake. To Petna Ndaliko Katondolo, for the ways his art and wisdom inspire me to live according to a worldview that actually sustains life.

And to the hostages—spirit, purpose, the creative force of chaos, and the perpetual awareness of the relationship between cause and effect—for actually sustaining life.

Notes

PREFACE

Epigraph following: Ralph Ellison, *Invisible Man* (New York: Vintage, 1995), 306.

1 *Transcend Exhibition Catalogue*, 2019, Yole!Africa Archives, Goma, Democratic Republic of the Congo.

2. TO SEE NSALA'S DAUGHTER

1 Ralph Ellison, *Invisible Man* (New York: Vintage, 1995), 13.

3. TO DECOMPOSE

1 Patricia J. Williams, *The Alchemy of Race and Rights* (Cambridge, MA: Harvard University Press, 1991), 216.

2 Toni Morrison, *Beloved* (New York: Knopf, 1987), 274.

3 I invoke here Christina Sharpe's multilayered notion of wake: "the keeping watch with the dead, the path of a ship, a consequence of something, in the line of flight and/or sight, awakening, and consciousness." Christina Sharpe, *In the Wake: On Blackness and Being* (Durham, NC: Duke University Press, 2016), 17–18 (see also 21).

4 Frantz Fanon, *Black Skin, White Masks* (New York: Grove, 1991), 82–108.

5 Ralph Ellison, *Invisible Man* (New York: Vintage, 1995), 36.

4. TO REPLICATE

1 W. E. B. Du Bois, *The Souls of Black Folks* (New York: Vintage, 1990), 8.

2 Paul Gilroy, "Diaspora," *Paragraph* 17, no. 3 (1994): 207–12.

3 Du Bois, *Souls of Black Folks*, 8.

4 Toni Morrison, *Beloved* (New York: Knopf, 1987), 274.

5 Patricia J. Williams, *The Alchemy of Race and Rights* (Cambridge, MA: Harvard University Press, 1991), 120.

5. TO CONTRADICT

1 As in previous chapters, I refer here to Sharpe's multiple notions of wake. Christina Sharpe, *In the Wake: On Blackness and Being* (Durham, NC: Duke University Press, 2016).

2 I pursue this line of thought in ways that echo Sylvia Wynter's argument in "1492: A New World View," in *Race, Discourse, and the Origin of the Americas: A New World View*, ed. Vera Lawrence Hyatt and Rex M. Nettleford (Washington, DC: Smithsonian Institution Press, 1995), 5–57.

3 David Livingstone, Lecture at the University of Cambridge, December 4, 1857, in *Dr. Livingstone's Cambridge Lectures*, ed. Rev. William Monk (London: Deighton, Bell, 1858), 165.

4 Henry Wellington Wack, speech at the First Meeting of the Belgian Committee of the International Association for the Exploration and Civilizing of Central Africa, in *The Story of the Congo Free State* (New York: G. P. Putnam's Sons, 1905), 15.

5 This summarizes numerous statements, including that of the Belgian parliamentary debate on the Congo Free State as well as of August Beernaert, former prime minister of Belgium (1884–1894) and recipient of the 1909 Nobel Peace Prize, who stated, "I must applaud the grandeur of the conception, the liberal and generous spirit with which Congo was admitted into the family of nations." *Verbatim Report of the Five Days' Congo Debate in the Belgian House of Representatives*, trans. E. D. Morel (Liverpool: John Richardson & Sons, 1906), 146.

6 W. E. B. Du Bois, *The Souls of Black Folks* (New York: Vintage, 1990), 8.

7 *The Congo: A Report of the Commission of Enquiry Appointed by the Congo Free State Government* (New York: G. P. Putnam's Sons, 1906), 166, 9–11.

8 Edmund D. Morel, *Affairs of West Africa* (London: William Heinemann, 1902), 328.

9 Roger Casement, *Correspondence and Report from His Majesty's Consul at Boma respecting the Administration of the Independent State of the Congo* (London: Printed for H. M. Stationery Office, by Harrison & Sons, 1904), 72.

10 J. A. Hobson, *Imperialism: A Study* (New York: James Pott & Co., 1902), 267.

11 *Loving v. Virginia*, 388 U.S. 1, 7 (1967).

12 "Act concerning Negroes and Other Slaves," *Proceedings and Acts of the General Assembly of Maryland* (September 1664): 534.

13 Laws of Virginia, 1662 Act XII; Latin added by William Henig, *The Statutes at Large* (1819). Cited in Jennifer Morgan, "*Partus sequitur ventrem*: Law, Race, and Reproduction in Colonial Slavery," *Small Axe* 22, no. 1 (March 2018): 1–17.

14 "An Act for Suppressing Outlying Slaves," in *The Statutes at Large: Being a Collection of All Laws of Virginia, from the First Session of the Legislature, in the Year 1619*, vol. 3, ed. William Waller Hening (Philadelphia: R. & W. & G. Bartow, 1823), 86.

15 "Act for Suppressing Outlying Slaves," 87.

16 U.S. Constitution, amend. 13, sec. 1.

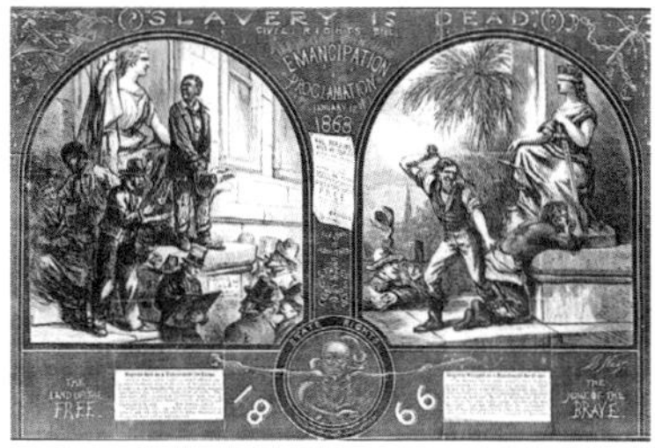

Note on *(?) Slavery Is Dead (?)* image in this chapter: The State Historical Society of Iowa web page for this image states: "Thomas Nast's 'Slavery Is Dead(?)' appeared in the January 12, 1867, edition of *Harper's Weekly*. Created five years after the Emancipation Proclamation, a year and two months after the ratification of the 13th Amendment and nine months after the passage of the Civil Rights Act of 1866, the image depicts the failure of each to fully protect African Americans. Two images, one depicting an African American being sold into slavery as punishment for a crime and a second depicting an African American being whipped as a punishment for a crime, draw attention to the ability of state governments to work around those three legal acts." "'Slavery Is Dead(?),' January 12, 1867," Iowa Department of Cultural Affairs, accessed April 20, 2022, https://iowaculture.gov/history/education/educator-resources/primary-source-sets/reconstruction/slavery-dead.

The society provides transcriptions of the text within the piece (see https://iowaculture.gov/sites/default/files/history-education-pss-reconstruction-slaverydead-transcription.pdf). Below the title, between the two images, the text reads: "CIVIL RIGHTS BILL EMANCIPATION PROCLAMATION JANUARY 1st 1863. All Persons Held As Slaves Within Any States Or Designated Part of a State, The People Whereof Shall Then be in Rebellion Against the United States, Shall be Then, Thenceforward, and Forever Free; and the Executive Government of the United States, including the military and naval authority thereof, will recognize and maintain the freedom of such persons, and will do no act or acts to repress such persons, or any of them, in any efforts they may make for their actual freedom. A Lincoln SLAVERY IS ABOLISHED BY THE STATES AND U.S. CONGRESS."

Below the image on the left, the text reads: "Negroes Sold as a Punishment for Crime. 'PUBLIC SALE.—The undersigned will offer for sale, at the Court-house door in the City of Annapolis, at 11 o'clock A.M., on Saturday, the 22d of December, a negro man named Jno. Johnson, aged about 40 years. The said negro was convicted at the October term, 1866, of the Circuit Court of Ann Arundel County, of larceny, and sentenced to be sold. WM. BRYAN, Sheriff.' 'BALTIMORE, DEC. 24—Four negroes convicted of larceny, and ordered to be sold by Judge Magruder, at Annapolis, were sold on Saturday last.'"

Below the image on the right, the text reads: "Negroes Whipped as a Punishment for Crime. 'On Monday last an order issued by Gen. Sickles, commanding this Department, was handed to Judge Fowle, by order of the Military Commander here, prohibiting infliction of corporal punishment. On Thursday a telegram from Gov. Worth, at Washington, was received by the same Judge, saying 'that the order was rescinded—you may proceed with the punishment. Sheriff Ray then proceeded to inflict the punishment.'—Raleigh (North Carolina) Standard of December 22, 1866."

17 U.S. Constitution, amend. 14, sec. 1.

18 In 1881, Tony Pace (a Black man) and Mary Cox (a white woman) were arrested and charged with living "in a state of adultery or fornication" because their sexual relationship violated Alabama's anti-miscegenation statute. They were both sentenced to two years' imprisonment in the state penitentiary in 1882. Pace appealed the case to Alabama's Supreme Court, arguing it conflicted with the Fourteenth Amendment, which declares no state shall deny to any person equal protection of the laws. The Alabama Supreme Court upheld the convictions because the punishment for interracial cohabitation was focused not "against the person of any particular color or race, but against the offense, the nature of which is determined by the opposite color of the cohabiting parties." In the eyes of the court, the "evil tendency" was greater in that kind of relationship than if both defendants were of the same race, since it could lead to "a mongrel population and a degraded civilization." On further appeal, the Supreme Court of the United States ruled that the criminalization of interracial sex did not violate the equal protection clause of the Fourteenth Amendment because whites and nonwhites were punished in equal measure for the offense of engaging in interracial sex. *Pace v. State of Alabama* 106 U.S. 583 (1883).

19 "An Act to Preserve Racial Integrity [SB 219]," in *Acts Passed at a General Assembly of the Commonwealth of Virginia* (Richmond, VA: Superintendent of Public Printing, 1924), 534–35.

20 *Loving v. Virginia*, 388 U.S. 1, 3 (1967).

21 *Loving v. Virginia.*

22 On July 31, 2008, the Massachusetts legislature voted to repeal a 1913 law (Massachusetts General Laws Chapter 207, Section 11) that invalidated marriages of non–state residents if their marriage was not permitted in their home state. This law was enacted during the height of anti-miscegenation sentiment but was repealed as part of the legal fight for same-sex marriage. In October 2008, a conservative group petitioned for a referendum to reinstate the law, though they failed to gather sufficient signatures.

23 As of September 2019, Alabama, Connecticut, Delaware, Kentucky, Louisiana, Minnesota, and Virginia required couples to identify their race in order to obtain a marriage license. This law was repealed in Virginia in October 2019.

24 Du Bois, *Souls of Black Folks*, 7.

25 James Baldwin, *Nobody Knows My Name* (New York: Dell, 1962), 19. "He is a Negro, of course, from the remarkable legal point of view which obtains in the United States, but more importantly . . . he was a Negro by choice and by depth of involvement—by experience in fact."

26 On September 18, 1858, in the fourth debate between Abraham Lincoln and Stephen Douglas in the Illinois race for the U.S. Senate in 1858, at Charleston, Illinois, Lincoln made his position on racial equality clear: "I will say then that I am not, nor ever have been, in favor of bringing about in any way the social and political equality of the white and black races; that I am not, nor have I ever been in favor of making voters of the negros, or jurors, or qualifying them to hold office, or having them to marry with white people. I will say in addition that there is a physical difference between the white and black races, which I suppose, will for ever forbid to [*sic*] two races living together upon terms of social and political equality, and, inasmuch, as they cannot so live, that while they do remain together, there must be the position of superior and inferior, that I as much as any other man an in favor of the superior position being assigned to the white man." Abraham Lincoln and Stephen A. Douglas, *Speeches of Douglas and Lincoln: Delivered at Charleston, Ill., Sept. 18th, 1858*, Democratic campaign publication reprinted from *Weekly Chicago Times*, September 23, 1858.

27 Lincoln first publicly advocated for colonization in 1852, and in 1854 said that his first instinct would be "to free all the slaves, and send them to Liberia" (the African state founded by the American Colonization Society in 1821). Abraham Lincoln and Stephen Arnold Douglas, *The First Lincoln and Douglas Debate: At Ottawa, Ill., Aug. 21, 1858* (Boston: Directors of the Old South Work, 1897), 15.

Nearly a decade later, even as he edited the draft of the preliminary Emancipation Proclamation in August 1862, Lincoln hosted a delegation of freed slaves at the White House in the hopes of getting their support on a plan for colonization in Central America. On December 31, 1862, the same day he finalized the Emancipation Proclamation, he signed a contract with Bernard Kock to ship approximately five thousand African Americans to a small island off Haiti's coast, using federal funds. See M. Vorenberg, "Abraham Lincoln and the Politics of Black Colonization," *Journal of the Abraham Lincoln Association* 14, no. 2 (1993): 22–45.

28 Patricia Williams, *The Alchemy of Race and Rights* (Cambridge, MA: Harvard University Press, 1991), 139.

6. TO CREATE

1 Patricia Williams, *The Alchemy of Race and Rights* (Cambridge, MA: Harvard University Press, 1992), 129–30. Quote continues: "To survive the transgression is terrifying and addictive. To know that everything has changed and yet that nothing has changed; and in leaping the chasm of the impossible division of self, a discovery of the self surviving, still well, still strong, and, as a curious consequence, renewed."

2 Boaventura de Sousa Santos, *Epistemologies of the South: Justice against Epistemicide* (New York: Routledge, 2016), 34.

3 I draw here on Ngũgĩ wa Thiong'o's notion of re-membering, in particular

his point that "creative imagination is one of the greatest of re-membering practices. The relationship of writers to their social memory is central to [this] mission. Memory is the link between the past and the present, between space and time, and it is the base of our dreams." Ngũgĩ wa Thiong'o, *Something Torn and New: An African Renaissance* (New York: BasicCivitas, 2009), 39.

4 This term was coined during a workshop on Decomposing the Colonial Gaze in Goma, DRC, when Lingala- and Kinyarwanda-speaking participants realized the similarities in their cultures' conceptions of time, which are suppressed by the imposition of European languages and laws that put neighboring groups in conflict. In defiance of these languages and laws, the term *ejo lobi* is a gesture of re-membering indigenous conceptions that pre-date (and to some extent survived) the big jagged lines that tether people and languages to nations-at-odds.

5 "The word of law, whether statutory or judge-made, is a subcategory of the underlying social motives and beliefs from which it is born. It is the technical embodiment of attempts to order society according to the consensus of ideals. When a society loses sight of those ideals and grants obeisance to words alone, law becomes sterile and formalistic. . . . A sort of punitive literalism ensues that leads to a high degree of thoughtless conformity; for literalism has, as one of its primary underlying values, order." Williams, *Alchemy of Race and Rights*, 138–39.

6 I echo here Christina Sharpe's reminder of the many "reappearances of the slave ship in everyday life in the form of the prison, the camp, and the school." Christina Sharpe, *In the Wake: On Blackness and Being* (Durham, NC: Duke University Press, 2016), 21.

7. TO LOVE NSALA'S DAUGHTER

1 1 Corinthians 13:4.

2 Middleton A. Harris, Morris Levitt, Roger Furman, and Ernest Smith, eds, *The Black Book*, with a foreword and preface by Toni Morrison (New York: Random House, 2009), 10.

Bibliography

"Act concerning Negroes and Other Slaves." *Proceedings and Acts of the General Assembly of Maryland* (September 1664): 533–34.

"An Act for Suppressing Outlying Slaves." In *The Statutes at Large: Being a Collection of All Laws of Virginia, from the First Session of the Legislature, in the Year 1619*, vol. 3, edited by William Waller Hening, 86–88. Philadelphia: R. & W. & G. Bartow, 1823.

"An Act to Preserve Racial Integrity [SB 219]." In *Acts Passed at a General Assembly of the Commonwealth of Virginia*, 534–35. Richmond, VA: Superintendent of Public Printing, 1924.

Baldwin, James. *Nobody Knows My Name*. New York: Dell, 1962.

Casement, Roger. *Correspondence and Report from His Majesty's Consul at Boma respecting the Administration of the Independent State of the Congo*. London: Printed for H. M. Stationery Office, by Harrison & Sons, 1904.

The Congo: A Report of the Commission of Enquiry Appointed by the Congo Free State Government. New York: G. P. Putnam's Sons, 1906.

Davies, Surekha. *Renaissance Ethnography and the Invention of the Human: New Worlds, Maps and Monsters*. Cambridge: Cambridge University Press, 2016.

Du Bois, W. E. B. *The Souls of Black Folks*. New York: Vintage, 1990.

Ellison, Ralph. *Invisible Man*. New York: Vintage, 1995.

Fanon, Frantz. *Black Skin, White Masks*. Translated by Charles Lam Markmann. New York: Grove, 1991.

Gilroy, Paul. "Diaspora." *Paragraph* 17, no. 3 (1994): 207–12.

Harris, Middleton A., Morris Levitt, Roger Furman, and Ernest Smith, eds. *The Black Book*. With a foreword and preface by Toni Morrison. New York: Random House, 2009.

Hobson, J. A. *Imperialism: A Study*. New York: James Pott & Co., 1902.

Lincoln, Abraham, and Stephen Arnold Douglas. *The First Lincoln and Douglas Debate: At Ottawa, Ill., Aug. 21, 1858*. Boston: Directors of the Old South Work, 1897.

Lincoln, Abraham, and Stephen A. Douglas. *Speeches of Douglas and Lincoln: Delivered at Charleston, Ill., Sept. 18th, 1858.* Democratic campaign publication reprinted from *Weekly Chicago Times*, September 23, 1858.

Livingstone, David. *Dr Livingstone's Cambridge Lectures: Together with a Prefatory Letter by the Rev. Professor Sedgwick.* Edited by William Monk. Cambridge: Deighton, Bell, 1858.

Morel, E. D. *Affairs of West Africa.* London: W. Heinemann, 1902.

Morgan, Jennifer. "*Partus sequitur ventrem*: Law, Race, and Reproduction in Colonial Slavery." *Small Axe* 22, no. 1 (2018): 1–17.

Morrison, Toni. *Beloved.* New York: Knopf, 1987.

Netzloff, Mark. "Lines of Amity: The Law of Nations in the Americas." In *Cultural Diplomacy and Literary Writing in the Early Modern World*, 54–68. New York: Oxford University Press, 2019.

Ngũgĩ wa Thiong'o. *Something Torn and New: An African Renaissance.* New York: BasicCivitas, 2009.

Santos, Boaventura de Sousa. *Epistemologies of the South: Justice against Epistemicide.* New York: Routledge, 2016.

Sharpe, Christina. *In the Wake: On Blackness and Being.* Durham, NC: Duke University Press, 2016.

Verbatim Report of the Five Days' Congo Debate in the Belgian House of Representatives. Translated by E. D. Morel. Liverpool: John Richardson & Sons, 1906.

Vorenberg, Michael. "Abraham Lincoln and the Politics of Black Colonization." *Journal of the Abraham Lincoln Association* 14, no. 2 (Summer 1993): 22–45.

Wack, Henry Wellington. *The Story of the Congo Free State: Social, Political, and Economic Aspects of the Belgian System of Government in Central Africa.* New York: G. P. Putnam's Sons, 1905.

Williams, Patricia J. *The Alchemy of Race and Rights.* Cambridge, MA: Harvard University Press, 1991.

Wynter, Sylvia. "1492: A New World View." In *Race, Discourse, and the Origin of the Americas: A New World View*, edited by Vera L. Hyatt and Rex Nettleford, 5–57. Washington, DC: Smithsonian Institution Press, 1995.

Index

Note: Page numbers in italics indicate illustrations.

Illustration Credits

1. ELEGY FOR NSALA

The Alice Seeley Harris Archive, Antislavery International and the Bodleian Library, University of Oxford, MSS. Brit. Emp. S. 17.

3. TO DECOMPOSE

FIGURES ON PAGE 11

Virunga Market pop-up exhibit, July 2016. Photograph by author.

SKM Station pop-up exhibit, July 2017. Photograph by author.

FIGURES ON PAGE 12

Mabanga Terminus exhibition, July 2019. Photograph by author.

Cap Kivu exhibition, July 2018. Photograph by author.

FIGURE ON PAGES 14–15

The Alice Seeley Harris Archive, Antislavery International and the Bodleian Library, University of Oxford, MSS. Brit. Emp. S. 17.

FIGURES ON PAGE 17

The Alice Seeley Harris Archive, Antislavery International and the Bodleian Library, University of Oxford, MSS. Brit. Emp. S. 17.

FIGURES ON PAGE 18

Replicate: Untitled 6. Photograph. Result of the Decomposing the Colonial Gaze workshop in Lubumbashi, Democratic Republic of the Congo, 2017. Reproduced with permission from Yole!Africa.

FIGURES ON PAGE 20

Petna Ndaliko Katondolo and M. Castofas, *Replicate: Mirror*. Photograph. Kinshasa, Democratic Republic of the Congo, 2020. Reproduced with permission from Alkebu Film Productions.

FIGURES ON PAGE 21

Contradict: Alone. Photograph. Result of the Decomposing the Colonial Gaze workshop in Lubumbashi, Democratic Republic of the Congo, 2018. Reproduced with permission from Yole!Africa.

Contradict: Untitled 14. Photograph. Result of the Decomposing the Colonial Gaze workshop in Lubumbashi, Democratic Republic of the Congo, 2018. Reproduced with permission from Yole!Africa.

FIGURE ON PAGE 22

The Alice Seeley Harris Archive, Antislavery International and the Bodleian Library, University of Oxford, MSS. Brit. Emp. S. 17.

FIGURE ON PAGE 23

Contradict: Untitled 9. Photograph. Result of Decomposing the Colonial Gaze workshop in Lubumbashi, Democratic Republic of the Congo, 2018. Reproduced with permission from Yole!Africa.

FIGURES ON PAGE 24

Petna Ndaliko Katondolo and M. Castofas, *Contradict: Mirror.* Photograph. Kinshasa, Democratic Republic of the Congo, 2020. Reproduced with permission from Alkebu Film Productions.

FIGURE ON PAGE 25

Abedi Mohamed, *Provisional Liberty*. Photograph. Result of the Decomposing the Colonial Gaze workshop in Goma, Democratic Republic of the Congo, 2018. Reproduced with permission from Yole!Africa.

FIGURES ON PAGE 26

Benin Butatunda, *At the Border*. Photograph. Result of the Decomposing the Colonial Gaze workshop in Goma, Democratic Republic of the Congo, 2018. Reproduced with permission from Yole!Africa.

Petna Ndaliko Katondolo, *Remains.* Photograph. Goma, Democratic Republic of the Congo, 2017. Reproduced with permission from Alkebu Film Productions.

FIGURE ON PAGE 27

Petna Ndaliko Katondolo, *Time.* Photograph. Goma, Democratic Republic of the Congo, 2017. Reproduced with permission from Alkebu Film Productions.

4. TO REPLICATE

FIGURES ON PAGE 33

Nzanzu Boboy, *João.* Oil on canvas. Goma, Democratic Republic of the Congo, 2020. Reproduced with permission from Alkebu Film Productions.

Nzanzu Boboy, *Léopold.* Oil on canvas. Goma, Democratic Republic of the Congo, 2020. Reproduced with permission from Alkebu Film Productions.

Petna Ndaliko Katondolo, *Heads of State.* Mixed media. Chapel Hill, United States, 2020. Reproduced with permission from Alkebu Film Productions.

FIGURES ON PAGE 37

Family photographs reproduced with permission of author.

FIGURES ON PAGE 39

Psalter (The Map Psalter) with added miniatures [map: hand colored]. Ca. 1262. Western Manuscripts. British Library, Add MS 28681, ff.9. https://www.amdigital.co.uk/about/blog/item/medieval-world-maps.

Detail from *Psalter (The Map Psalter) with added miniatures* [map: hand colored]. Ca. 1262. Western Manuscripts. British Library, Add MS 28681, ff.9.

FIGURE ON PAGE 40

Opicinus de Canistris, detail from *Canistris Maps* [map]. 1341. Biblioteca Apostalica Vaticana, Rome, Italy. http://www.henry-davis.com/MAPS/LMwebpages/230B.html.

FIGURES ON PAGE 41

Claudius Ptolemy and Lienhart Holle, *Beatissimo Patri Paulo Secundo Pontificic Maximo. Donis Nicolaus Germanus* [map: hand colored]. 1482. British Library, IC. 9304.

Willem Janszoon Blaeu, *Nova Totius Terrarum Orbis Geographica Ac Hydrographica Tabula auct Guiljelmo Blaeuw*, 1630. Amsterdam. The Barry Lawrence Ruderman Map Collection, Stanford Libraries. purl.stanford.edu/fh550gt3106.

FIGURE ON PAGE 42

Abraham Ortelius, *Orbis Terrarum Tabula Recens Emendata et in Lucen Edita* [map: hand colored]. ca. 1663. Library of Congress.

FIGURES ON PAGE 43

Map Showing the Distribution of the Slave Population of the Southern States of the United States [map]. 1861. Norman B. Leventhal Map Center Collection, Boston Public Library. https://ark.digitalcommonwealth.org/ark:/50959/w9505r836.

Plan d'Elizabethville et Environs [map]. 1927. Figure 4 in Stéphanie Perazzone, "Congo: A State Ecosystem" (PhD diss., Ghent University, 2018).

FIGURES ON PAGE 45

Chérie N. Rivers and Nzanzu Boboy, *Replicate: Nsala's Daughter.* Photograph and oil on canvas. Goma, Democratic Republic of the Congo, 2020. Reproduced with permission from Alkebu Film Productions.

5. TO CONTRADICT

FIGURE ON PAGE 47

Nzanzu Boboy, *Ina Kale.* Oil on canvas. Goma, Democratic Republic of the Congo, 2020. Reproduced with permission from Alkebu Film Productions.

FIGURES ON PAGES 49–52

The Alice Seeley Harris Archive, Antislavery International and the Bodleian Library, University of Oxford, MSS. Brit. Emp. S. 17.

FIGURE ON PAGE 54

Myron H. Kimball, *Emancipated Slaves Brought from Louisiana by Colonel George H. Banks*, December 1863. Albumen silver print from glass negative, 13.2 × 18.3 cm. Gillman Collection, Purchase, The Horace W. Goldsmith Foundation Gift, through Joyce and Robert Menschel, 2005.

FIGURE ON PAGE 55

Unidentified artist, *Virginian Luxuries*, ca. 1825. Oil on canvas. Colonial Williamsburg Foundation.

FIGURES ON PAGE 56 (TOP TO BOTTOM)

Myron H. Kimball, *Isaac & Rosa, Slave Children from New Orleans,* ca. 1863. Photographic print on carte-de-visite mount, albumen, 10 × 6 cm. Library of Congress.

Kissing Couple from cover page of *What Miscegenation Is! and What We Are to Expect Now That Mr. Lincoln Is Re-elected*, by L. Seaman. Illustration. New York: Waller & Willetts, 1865. Cornell University Library, Division of Rare and Manuscript Collections.

Thomas Nast, *(?) Slavery Is Dead (?)*, United States, 1867. Print: wood engraving, 40 × 27 cm. Library of Congress.

FIGURES ON PAGE 57 (TOP TO BOTTOM; LEFT TO RIGHT)

Thomas Nast, *The Union as It Was, the Lost Cause, Worse than Slavery*, 1874. Print: wood engraving. Library of Congress.

Virginia Department of Health, cover of *The Racial Integrity Act* as published in the *Virginia Health Bulletin, March 1924*. University of Virginia Special Collections.

Virginia Department of Health, *Registration of Birth and Color, 1924*. Rockbridge County (Va.) Clerk's Correspondence [Walter A. Plecker to A. T. Shields], 1912–1943. Local Government Records Collection, Rockbridge County Court Records. Library of Virginia, Richmond, Virginia.

FIGURES ON PAGE 58 (TOP TO BOTTOM; LEFT TO RIGHT)

Anti-integration Propaganda Flyer, ca. 1958. Arkansas History Commission, Jim Johnson Collection.

Poster in Gary Yankers, *Prop Art: Over 1,000 Contemporary Political Posters* (New York: Darien House, 1972), 188, fig. 756.

John T. Bledsoe, *Little Rock, Rally at State Capitol*. Photograph. Little Rock, Arkansas, 1959. Library of Congress.

Robert E. Lee, for the N.C. Bar Association. "NC Prohibits Any Marriage between Races," *Rocky Mount, N.C. Telegram*, November 10, 1963, 7A. Microfilm, Wilson Library, University of North Carolina at Chapel Hill.

FIGURE ON PAGE 59

Screenshot of "'Aryan' and 'Octoroon': Couples Challenge Racial Labels to Get Married in Virginia: The State Mandates Would-Be Brides and Grooms List Their Race to Obtain a Marriage License." Rachel Weiner, *Washington Post*, September 6, 2019.

FIGURES ON PAGE 62 (LEFT TO RIGHT)

The Alice Seeley Harris Archive, Antislavery International and the Bodleian Library, University of Oxford, MSS. Brit. Emp. S. 17.

J. Waeshle, *Emancipation of the Slaves, Proclamed [i.e. Proclaimed] on the 22nd September, by Abraham Lincoln, President of the United States of North America*. Print: lithograph. Philadelphia, ca. 1862. Library of Congress.

FIGURES ON PAGE 63

Chérie N. Rivers and Nzanzu Boboy, *Contradict: Nsala's Daughter.* Photograph and oil on canvas. Goma, Democratic Republic of the Congo, 2021. Reproduced with permission from Alkebu Film Productions.

6. TO CREATE

FIGURE ON PAGE 67

The Alice Seeley Harris Archive, Antislavery International and the Bodleian Library, University of Oxford, MSS. Brit. Emp. S. 17.

FIGURE ON PAGE 71

Petna Ndaliko Katondolo, *Ejo Lobi.* Mixed media. Yira land, 2020. Reproduced with permission from Alkebu Film Productions.

FIGURE ON PAGE 73

Petna Ndaliko Katondolo, *From.* Mixed media. Yira land, 2020. Reproduced with permission from Alkebu Film Productions.

FIGURES ON PAGE 75

Family correspondence, reproduced with permission from author.

FIGURE ON PAGE 77

Chérie N. Rivers and Petna Ndaliko Katondolo, *Colonial Logic.* Yira land, 2020. Reproduced with permission from Alkebu Film Productions.

FIGURE ON PAGE 78

Petna Ndaliko Katondolo, *Orphaned Wondering.* Mixed media. Yira land, 2020. Reproduced with permission from Alkebu Film Productions.

FIGURES ON PAGE 79

Chérie N. Rivers and Petna Ndaliko Katondolo, *Create: Nsala's Daughter.* Mixed media. Yira land, 2021. Reproduced with permission from Alkebu Film Productions.

7. TO LOVE NSALA'S DAUGHTER

FIGURE ON PAGE 84

Thomas Satterwhite Noble, *The Modern Medea—the Story of Margaret Garner Margaret Garner, a Slave Who Escaped from Kentucky to Ohio; Her 4 Children, 2 of Which She Killed So They Would Not Have to Endure Slavery, Lying Dead on Floor; and 4 Men Who Pursued Her.* 1867. Print: wood engraving, 27.6 × 40.3 cm. Library of Congress.

FIGURE ON PAGE 87

Petna Ndaliko Katondolo, *Nyamuhange Apipawe!* Mixed media. Yira land, 2020. Reproduced with permission from Alkebu Film Productions.